MISTAKES AUTHORS MAKE

Rave Reviews

"I LOVE the book so far! Clear-concise-comprehensive with practical info the aspiring author needs!"

—**Laura Venecia Rodriguez**, Author
Yoga at Home: Gain Energy, Flexibility, and Serenity in 20-30 Minutes a Day

"*Mistakes Authors Make* features 50 of the most common errors book authors make in writing, publishing and promoting their books. All of them should be corrected. Correct one mistake a day and within two months, you'll be far ahead of most book authors. You'll be surprised how quickly you can sell more books when you fix these errors. Start today!"

—**John Kremer**, Author
1001 Ways to Market Your Books

"Rick Frishman is my go-to guy for book publicity and marketing. I trust him deeply and he's earned his reputation as an expert, a creative confidante, and the best book publicist in the nation."

— **Brendon Burchard**, Author
Life's Golden Ticket

"*Mistakes Authors Make* is a must-read for new and experienced authors alike! Sadly, I made at least 16 of the mistakes in the first 11 books I authored. This easy-to-read book would have saved me countless hours and headaches starting out. I wish I had mentors like Rick, Bret and Bryan who share on these pages everything you need to succeed. The practical tools make it crystal clear how to avoid pitfalls and lead you to mega-success!"

— **Phil Johncock**, The Grant Professor
PhilJohncock.com

"If you want to write a book or make sure that your book is a smashing success read this now and take action! You'll be amazed at the difference it will make in your success!

— **John Assaraf**, New York Times Bestselling Author
The Answer and *Having It All*
CEO, Praxis Now

"This book is a MUST READ for anyone thinking of writing a book, in the process of writing a book, or having already published a book in any format. The mistakes AND solutions to those mistakes discussed in this book will save you so much time and money. In fact, I think it will MAKE you more money due to the elements you may not have thought about yet. I'm checking some of these tips against my book that's already published and going through this book again for the book I'm currently working on. Do yourself a favor and go ahead and get this book right now – you won't regret it."

— **Frank E. Deardurff III** – That One Web Guy!
Coauthor of *"The 50 Biggest Website Mistakes"*

Rick Frishman is one of only ten people who understand and have mastered the book publishing process – I have counseled with him, listened to him, and watched the books he promoted turn to gold. If you're looking for someone to take your book to the promised land, I promise that Rick Frishman is the rocket ship that will take you there.

— **Jeffrey Gitomer**, *King, Buy Gitomer, Inc.*

Bret Ridgway is an information marketer's best friend. Bret is great because he really likes the business. He understands the business. He's IN the business. He's an author and an information publisher himself. And, he really cares about you. He really gets to know what you're doing and looks for ways to give you what you want, what you've asked for, and also to improve upon the process. He will help you take what you're doing to the next level.

— **David Garfinkel**, Author
Breakthrough Copywriting

Rick Frishman is one of the most well-connected people I know. He understands every aspect of author promotion and is able to deliver exactly what the individual project requires. His strategic thinking skills, his deep understanding of what really delivers, and his collaborative and positive personal style make Rick and his team a perfect choice for publishers and authors alike. Highly recommended.

— **Cindy Ratzlaff**, V.P., Associate Publisher,
Rodale Books

"As an author of multiple ebooks and a soon-to-be-published hard copy book, this book covers everything across the spectrum from the conceptual to publication and sales. I would strongly recommend reading this book regardless of where you are at in your publishing endeavors. You'll be better off and likely avoid a large number of costly (both time and financial) mistakes."

— **James Bogash**, DC
Chiropractic Physician

Rick Frishman is a genius when it comes to publicity. If you need someone to help you get into the media he's the go-to guy. And he's a great guy!

— **Ellen Violette**, ebook/Internet Coach, Author and Copywriter,
Create A Splash, LLC, /The ebook Coach

Rick Frishman was "the go to guy" if you wanted to publicize your book or project two decades ago. Well, now he is an industry leader in the same category. Rick knows how to get eyes and ears on your project. He's still the go to guy.

— **Jim Cathcart**, President & Founder
Catchart Institute, Inc.

Rick Frishman is without a doubt one of the top book publicists in the country. Not only has he represented many bestselling authors as the founder of Planned Television Arts, he has mentored hundreds of emerging authors and professional speakers including myself with his stellar workshops. Rick is truly a professional of the highest caliber and someone I am product to call a colleague and friend. December 4, 2008.

— **Robert Stack**, MCLC, APR, Fellow PRSA, Owner
Fame Coach

Learn How to Avoid the 50 Biggest...

MISTAKES
AUTHORS MAKE

Essential Steps for
Achieving Success as an Author

RICK FRISHMAN, BRET RIDGWAY, BRYAN HANE

New York

MISTAKES AUTHORS MAKE

Essential Steps for Achieving Success as an Author

Published in New York, New York, by Morgan James Publishing. Morgan James and The Entrepreneurial Publisher are trademarks of Morgan James, LLC. www.MorganJamesPublishing.com

The Morgan James Speakers Group can bring authors to your live event. For more information or to book an event visit The Morgan James Speakers Group at www.TheMorganJamesSpeakersGroup.com.

A **free** eBook edition is available with the purchase of this print book.

CLEARLY PRINT YOUR NAME ABOVE IN UPPER CASE

Instructions to claim your free eBook edition:
1. Download the BitLit app for Android or iOS
2. Write your name in **UPPER CASE** on the line
3. Use the BitLit app to submit a photo
4. Download your eBook to any device

ISBN 978-1-63047-457-7 paperback
ISBN 978-1-63047-458-4 eBook
ISBN 978-1-63047-459-1 hardcover
Library of Congress Control Number:
2014918658

Cover Design by:
Frank Deardurff
frank@deardurff.com

Interior Design by:
Bonnie Bushman
bonnie@caboodlegraphics.com

In an effort to support local communities and raise awareness and funds, Morgan James Publishing donates a percentage of all book sales for the life of each book to Habitat for Humanity Peninsula and Greater Williamsburg.

Get involved today, visit
www.MorganJamesBuilds.com

Habitat
for Humanity®
Peninsula and
Greater Williamsburg
Building Partner

Table of Contents

Acknowledgements

It's often that said that it takes a village to raise a child and the birthing and raising of a new book from concept to market requires a similar collaborative effort. Each of us offers sincere thanks to our coauthors and to David Hancock and his publishing team at Morgan James. The input from Jim Howard, Margo Toulouse and Bethany Marshall was invaluable in crafting a much better book for our readers.

Thanks also go out to Frank Deardurff for a great cover design and for putting up with our seemingly dozens of cover modifications as we moved along. Your patience and professionalism are most appreciated.

All three of us would like to thank our wives for well, putting up with each of us. To Robbi, Karen and Jessika, thank you for your continued support and for always being there for us.

Foreword

My love affair with books came at an early age, as my mother would read to me often and take me to the library for a stack of books. I recognized at an early age the power of the written word to evoke emotion, inspire others and, as a boy of eight or nine, to take me to magical places of adventure.

It was early in my business career that I first crossed paths with the three men who authored this book. Rick Frishman would prove to be an invaluable mentor as I launched my *New York Times* Bestseller *The AdSense Code*. Bret Ridgway and Bryan Hane and their team over at Speaker Fulfillment Services became a valued supplier and supporter when I created my first home study course and other products beyond my book.

Rick has probably forgotten more about book publicity than I'll ever know. The massive success of the legendary *Chicken Soup for the Soul* Series from Mark Victor Hansen and Jack Canfield was, in no small part, due to the efforts of Rick and his PR team. And, with their behind xvi | MISTAKES AUTHORS MAKE

the scenes work with many of the biggest names in the information marketing world, Bret and Bryan bring a unique perspective about the publishing world that can greatly benefit any author.

This new book from Rick, Bret and Bryan *Mistakes Authors Make* is a resource I wish I'd had available to me when I was writing my first book. Mainly because I made some of the mistakes in the book! But, more importantly, rather than just pointing out the mistakes is they teach you how to avoid these mistakes, greatly increasing your chances for success as an author.

The path of an author can be a tricky one to navigate and I wouldn't recommend that any one venture that path alone. Take advantage of the resources that are available to you that I wish I'd had at my fingertips when I was beginning my journey as an author. Rick, Bret and Bryan have penned a resource that should be part of any author's resource library.

Will you still make some mistakes as an author? Of course you will – you're human. But by minimizing your mistakes with the aid of valuable resources like the book you hold in your hands you can greatly increase your chances for success.

—**Joel Comm**

New York Times Bestselling Author of *The Adsense Code* and *Twitter Power 3.0: How to Dominate Your Market One Tweet at a Time*
www.JoelComm.com

Introduction

The road to success as an author can indeed be a bit challenging. There are so many aspects to authoring, publishing and marketing your book that it's easy for you to make critical mistakes that can take you off course and significantly decrease your chances for success. When you learn to avoid the biggest mistakes authors make you can greatly enhance your chances for success in the publishing world.

In this insider's look at the worlds of publishing and book marketing coauthors Rick Frishman, Bret Ridgway and Bryan Hane bring their combined 65 years of experience in the publishing world to you and share their secrets to success. You'll learn:

- How to master media and other key marketing channels authors should use
- Keys to capturing the browsing buyer in bookstores and online
- The new publishing landscape and how it impacts you

- How to increase the readability of your book so readers keep coming back
- How your book is the key piece of your own information marketing empire
- And much, much more

In all you'll find 50 key mistakes that authors make covered in this book. You'll learn not only about the book creation process, but also book marketing, the various publishing models, the business behind your book and more. We'll suggest various resources that can greatly benefit you as an author if you want to take your success to the next level.

Maybe you want to write a book to inspire others. Or maybe your reason is to teach others some specific tactics and strategies about your area of expertise. Regardless of your reason your story should be heard.

Without a doubt every business owner should have a book. Nothing establishes you as an expert in your niche more quickly than being the author of a book. It doesn't matter whether you're a chiropractor, lawyer, plumber, mortgage broker, butcher, baker or candlestick maker. Being an author is simply a "must have" in your marketing arsenal.

We wish you the greatest of success as an author and are pleased to provide you this resource to help you down the path. And we hope we'll cross paths with you at one of our Author 101 University live events sometime in the future.

All our best,

Rick, Bret and Bryan

Section 1

BEFORE YOU WRITE

Believing You Can't Write a Book

Everyone has a story to tell. Don't you? And whether the purpose of your story is to inspire, to entertain, to train, or to simply capture your history in words you need to tell your story. No one else in the entire history of mankind shares your story. It is truly unique and individual to you.

People love stories and the story you have to share can truly make a difference in the life of another person. If you don't tell your story—if you don't write your book—then you are both depriving others of the benefits of your knowledge and wisdom and you are depriving yourself of the satisfaction of having a positive impact on others.

If you're a business owner or a business professional your story can not only have a positive impact on others, it can also have a massive impact on the profitability of your business. Your book should be a major marketing force for you. Nothing establishes you better as an expert in your industry and as the go-to person people should work with than being the author of a book.

So what's stopping you? If the thought of staring at a blank sheet of paper or a blank page on your computer screen is overwhelming you're not alone. Many people who say they want to write a book can't seem to get the first actual word down on paper or on the screen. They are intimidated by the thought of the end goal and can't seem to understand that it's a step-by-step process.

You build it word by word, sentence by sentence, paragraph by paragraph, chapter by chapter. You don't write a book—you write a few words that become a few sentences that become a few paragraphs that become a few chapters. Then you combine these words and sentences and paragraphs and chapters together and suddenly you have a book.

That's easy for you to say you might be saying. You understand a book is something you build step by step but that doesn't make it any easier to get it started. Well, never fear, here are four others ways you can write your book without putting a pen to paper or your fingers to a keyboard.

#1 Talk Your Book

If the thought of typing out a book manuscript totally turns you off you might consider talking your book. Just get a decent USB microphone you can plug into your computer like the Audio-technica AT2020 or similar brand. We use the Audio-technica microphone and it has been great for us.

Just plug your microphone in, power up your recording software such as Sound Forge, Adobe Audition, or Garage Band and start talking. Then have someone transcribe your audio and provide you with a written document to work from. It beats starting with a blank sheet of paper for many people. Of course, you'll need to edit it and clean it up in some way, but it's easier for you to modify existing copy rather than create from scratch.

Here's another possibility. Author 101 Online co-founders Bryan Hane and Bret Ridgway do a weekly Blog Talk Radio show about information marketing. The audio recordings from previous episodes of the show can be transcribed, grouped accordingly and turned into a book. It's simply the repurposing of existing content into another format.

#2 Repurpose Articles or Blog Posts You Have Written

Maybe you're already a writer. Do you have articles you've written that have been distributed? Or maybe you're a long time blogger and have been sharing your wisdom via blog for many years. Can you combine articles or blog posts you've already written to make up the chapters of a book? Yes you can. And even if you don't have all the parts for an entire book you may well have a good chunk of it in content you've already created. Repurposing is powerful, use it.

#3 Have Someone Interview You

This is essentially another form of "talking your book". If you need interaction with another person to really get your juices flowing rather than talking into a microphone by yourself have someone conduct an interview of you. Give them a number of questions in advance you want them to ask you and then just turn on your recorder and let it roll. Take your recorded interview (or interviews) to a transcriber and have them turn it into a written document that's ready for your final touches.

#4 Hire a Ghostwriter

Maybe time is the biggest thing you battle to get your book done. You may want to consider flat out just paying someone else to write your book for you. That's fine, because you want to be an author and not a writer. And there is a big difference. Some of the most popular books in history were not written by the authors—they were ghostwritten. Just be aware that good ghostwriters are not easy to find and can be very expensive. So make sure you have a significant budget available for the writing process if you want to go the ghostwriter route.

So there are four different ways you can write a book without actually writing a book. And there are some other ways we haven't even mentioned that might also work. Do you have a live presentation from an event or TV appearance that someone can transcribe for you and you can use that to form the basis of a book?

Certainly, if you prefer to put the proverbial pen to paper or type it out yourself then great, go for it! Or, if one of the alternative methods of book writing better suits your needs then go for that.

"Your book doesn't have to be perfect,
it just has to be."
– Rick Frishman

You can be the author of the book. And recognition of the fact that that doesn't mean you have to be the one to write every single word of your book might be the first step to your finally starting to get that book done. Remember, it's the story that you want to share and there are multiple ways for you to write your book and to get your story told. In a sense it doesn't matter how you get it written—you just need to get it done. And, as Rick says, "Your book doesn't have to be perfect, it just has to be."

Writing a Book for the Wrong Reason

Almost every author dreams of writing a *New York Times* or Amazon Bestseller, receiving a large six or seven figure dollar advance and sitting back and enjoying the good life as the royalty checks roll in month after month after month. Snap out of it! If that describes you then you're probably writing your book for the wrong reason.

Does it happen? Yes it does. Does it happen often? Not so much. Now the bestseller part is achievable by many. "Bestseller" has become a manipulated term. You can drive traffic to Amazon to buy your book during a certain time frame and the sale of just a few hundred copies can put you on their bestseller lists.

And the last we heard it takes sales of about 9000 copies of a book in a one week period to hit one of the *New York Times* bestseller lists. Not insignificant, but doable by many. But leveraging that bestseller status on Amazon or on the *New York Times* list into large advances and mega-royalties is far, far trickier to achieve.

Bottom line, if you're writing a book for the purpose of making a lot of money from direct sales of the book it's time to recalibrate and think about things a little differently. Here's what we mean.

First and foremost, your wanting to share your unique story with the world should be your primary driving force. We talked about this in the previous chapter. Then, with a well-written book and a great on-going marketing campaign you have an opportunity to turn your book into a money maker. But the money made in nearly every case is not the money made directly from book sales. It's the money made from the things that you have to offer to people that are beyond the book.

Maybe it's a coaching program. Maybe it's a membership site where you regularly add new content for those that want to follow you. Maybe it's live events where people come to hear your message from stage. Or maybe it's a home study course and other higher ticket information products that people can purchase from you. For the advanced book marketer it may be several of these.

The point is that you need to determine, in advance, what is the end game of your book. How are you going to leverage your book to have an even wider impact on the world than you can with a book alone? It's those back end products and services you have to offer where the real money is made in almost every case.

"Your book is a door opener"

Your book is a door opener. It's an introduction to you and your message. It's a marketing weapon in your arsenal as you look to build your platform and increase your reach to the world. If you happen to make some money on the direct sales of your book that is wonderful.

You should consider that a bonus. The smart book marketer recognizes that the real money is in what the book can do for you in terms of opening doors and making opportunities available.

In today's world the term "author" still has a certain cache', a reverence associated with it that you can parlay into bigger and better things. If you want to be known as an authority or an expert in your field then having a book is simply a must. Having that book gives you credibility that may be difficult to achieve otherwise. Because you have "authored" a book (you notice we didn't say written) you are the expert, you are the authority to which people should pay attention.

You can't have nearly as much impact as you want to have if you have a book, and only a book, to offer people. Many authors have really fumbled the ball on this one. They poured their heart and soul into creating a great book, put a fantastic marketing campaign behind it and achieved bestseller status. Maybe they even made a little money on book sales directly. But, they hadn't given any up front thought to what their end game was. Plus they hadn't taken the time to put into place in advance their follow-up products or services that their book buyers could take advantage of. They left so much money on the table it was a tragedy. A wasted opportunity.

We are not saying that if you want to write a book just for the purposes of sharing your story with a few family members and close friends you can't do that. If your goal isn't to positively impact as many people as possible then, by all means, write your book, print off a few copies and hand them out to those you want. That's a wonderful legacy for you.

But, if you have a message you want to share with as much of the world as possible you do need to give forethought to how you can leverage your book to have an even wider impact. Does that mean more work? Of course it does. Why? Because you're not necessarily writing only a book. You may also have to simultaneously be developing the other products and services that will make up your follow-up offering that your book will help to drive sales of.

Being the author of a book is a wonderful thing. Just be sure you are authoring your book for the right reason. Your book can open up opportunities for you that may not have been available otherwise if you didn't have a book. It can introduce you to people that become your fans or followers or what legendary marketer Dan Kennedy likes to call "your herd". It can lead to the sales of higher priced products and services where some significant money can be made. It can open up speaking opportunities where you'll have the chance to get up on stage and share your message directly with larger groups.

Just don't do it because you think you're going to get rich on direct sales of your book. Not trying to burst your bubble—it does happen occasionally. But authoring a book for that reason alone is the wrong reason—and in almost all cases a one way ticket to failure.

No Real Understanding of Your Target Market

We can't count the number of times we've heard a new author say words to the effect of "Everybody needs to read my book. Everyone would benefit from it." Those, my friend, are words that point to a book that is, in all likelihood, going to fail in the marketplace.

Why? There's a common marketing phrase that says "If you try to sell to everybody you sell to nobody." If you think everyone needs your fantastic new gizmo you're kidding yourself because it makes it so hard to craft a message that really resonates with any particular group of people.

"If you try to sell to everybody you sell to nobody"

The same is true for your book. If you try to position it in your marketing message as something that everyone needs to read then it makes it hard for people to jump on board because they don't consider themselves everyone. You need to figure out what subset of everyone you can most positively impact with your message and focus your marketing efforts to that group. What is your ideal niche?

- Are your readers most likely to be male or female?
- What age range are they in?
- What is their ethnicity?
- Do they have specific geographical ties?
- Do they have a specific health issue they associate themselves with?
- Do they have a particular hobby they're involved with?

There is a common phrase in marketing these days called the "Marketing Avatar." A marketing avatar is a process of honing in on exactly who your perfect customer is. In your case, the perfect reader. This process entails detailing everything about this perfect reader, including gender, age, job, hobbies, trends, fears, desires, everything!

Very few authors make the effort to truly understand their ideal market in depth. Where do they hang out online? Are there forums or discussion boards online related to their interests and/or concerns that people hang out in? What keyword or keyword phrase are they using online to search for answers to their questions?

A keyword or keyword phrase is the word or group of words someone types into the search box in their browser to seek information. If you know what keyword phrase people commonly use that relates to the topic of your book you may have the basis for a great book title. As much as possible you want to put your book out there where people are already hanging out.

Go to your favorite search engine and type in a keyword phrase that would relate to the book you want to write and add the word "forum". It's pretty easy online to find groups talking about the things you want to write about. Look for recurring problems for which people are seeking solutions.

The late, great copywriter Gary Halbert was once asked what competitive advantage he'd want if he had hamburgers to sell. Was it the best location? Was it the best tasting burger? Was it the freshest buns? "None of the above," said Gary. What he'd want is a "starving crowd." So where is your "starving crowd"?

And, very importantly, who else is trying to serve that same crowd? What other books already exist in the marketplace targeting the niche you want to serve?

Here's a little exercise for you. Go to Amazon.com and type in the keyword phrase that you feel most accurately describes the book you want to write. In most cases page after page of results will come up. Start to look through those titles that come up on page one of the results. Then move on down to page two and so on and so forth.

What you're looking at are the book descriptions of those titles in your niche. What keyword phrases are they using? How are they trying to attract readers to their book? What words are used in the titles of their books? You can piggyback off the success of others.

You can even look at things like the fonts and colors that those books are using on their covers. It's not necessary to reinvent the wheel. Our good friend Armand Morin says "Success leaves traces." Look at the most successful books focused at the audience you want to serve and model their success.

Remember that if you have a message you want to share with as many people as possible then it is critical for you to have as much understanding of your marketplace as possible. If you're writing a book just because you want to share your story with just a few family members and friends then this is not so important. But if you want to have "massive impact" then make sure you take the time to understand your market inside and out.

This is especially true when you are trying to build a business off your book. You must recognize that the book is going to be your front end product and you know you need to have follow-up offerings of other products and services that will serve the market you want to serve. Just be sure you choose a market niche that is large enough in size to build a business on.

You could have a great passion for underwater wicker basket weaving. But if there aren't any other books on your subject and you can't find any online groups where people are talking about your subject then, chances are, you have a market that isn't large enough to build a business on. We're not saying you shouldn't write your book if that is truly your passion. Just recognize the money making limitations you face serving such a small niche.

Locating a great niche can be quite challenging. You want a targeted enough niche that your potential readers deeply associate themselves with that niche. That implies a smaller, more tightly-knit group. Yet you want a large enough niche that the size of the universe your book will appeal to is significant enough in size to support building a business on that niche. It's kind of a fine line that you walk.

Resist the urge to simply pour onto the page everything you know about your topic. Be sure to take the time to research the market and develop as clear of understanding as possible as to how you can best service that market.

Expecting Instant Success

We've all heard the phrase "overnight sensation" where someone, seemingly out of nowhere, emerges on to the scene to big fanfare. What most fail to realize is that that so-called instant success was a result of years of hard work that finally came to fruition.

Most first-time authors have the expectation of hitting it big and becoming the next big thing. And it should happen yesterday of course. And while you should have big expectations and you should definitely be prepared (as much as possible) for success don't be surprised and don't become too frustrated if it doesn't happen right out of the gate.

Michael Jordan is regarded by many as the greatest basketball player of all time. Yet, he was cut from his high school basketball team because he wasn't considered good enough. But he kept working at his game, improving his skills, and eventually he led the Chicago Bulls to 6 NBA titles.

According to buzzfeed.com Toni Morrison published her first novel at age 40 as a single mom. Morrison completed her first novel, *The Bluest Eye*, while she taught at Howard University and raised two children after a divorce. The novel tanked in sales and garnered mixed reviews. It was only in her mid-forties that *Sula* and *Song of Solomon* set her on the track of becoming the only recent American author to win a Nobel Prize.

Dorothy Allison was 42 when *Bastard Out of Carolina* came out. She had worked as a mop racker, waitress, nanny, feminist bookstore founder, maid, salad girl, Social Security clerk, rape crisis center phone counselor, and substitute teacher. She basically lived 12 lifetimes before she wrote a National Book Award-nominated novel.

George Saunders was an environmental engineer before he became a best-selling author. Though now hailed as one of the world's finest short story writers, he came to literature slantwise, after studying geophysical engineering at the Colorado School of Mines, then working as an oil surveyor in Sumatra, a doorman at Beverly Hills, a roofer in Chicago, and a knuckle-puller at a slaughterhouse. His first book, *CivilWarLand in Bad Decline*, was published when he was 37.

Contrary to what many would lead you to believe, a great deal of authors and other artists had their breakthroughs after their mid-thirties: Don DeLillo, Paul Cezanne, Cheryl Strayed, Sapphire, Phil Hartman, Lucille Ball, Zach Galifianakis, Edward Kelsey Moore, Laura Ingalls Wilder, Maya Angelou, Joseph Conrad, Paul Gaugin, Leonard Cohen, and others.

"Overnight sensations are generally years in the making"

It will take perseverance and hard work. Overnight successes are generally years in the making. But success can happen. LiteraryRejections. com recently offered up an extensive collection of the some of the biggest errors of judgment in publishing history. For their complete list visit http://www.literaryrejections.com/best-sellers-initially-rejected/.

After 5 years of continual rejection, the writer finally lands a publishing deal: Agatha Christie. Her book sales are now in excess of $2 billion. Only William Shakespeare has sold more.

The Christopher Little Literary agency receives 12 publishing rejections in a row for their new client, until the eight-year-old daughter of a Bloomsbury editor demands to read the rest of the book. The editor agrees to publish but advises the writer to get a day job since she has little chance of making money in children's books. Yet *Harry Potter and the Philosopher's Stone* by J.K. Rowling spawns a series where the last four novels consecutively set records as the fastest-selling books in history, on both sides of the Atlantic, with combined sales of 450 million.

Louis L'Amour received 200 rejections before Bantam took a chance on him. He is now their best ever selling author with 330 million sales.

"Too different from other juveniles on the market to warrant its selling." A rejection letter sent Dr. Seuss. 300 million sales and the 9th best-selling fiction author of all time.

"You have no business being a writer and should give up." Zane Grey ignores the advice. There are believed to be over 250 million copies of his books in print.

140 rejections stating *"Anthologies don't sell"* until the *Chicken Soup for the Soul* series by Jack Canfield and Mark Victor Hansen sells 125 million copies.

Having sold only 800 copies on its limited first release, the author finds a new publisher and *The Alchemist* by Paulo Coelho sells 75 million.

The Tale of Peter Rabbit by Beatrix Potter was rejected so many times she decided to self-publish 250 copies. It has now sold 45 million.

Margaret Mitchell gets 38 rejections from publishers before finding one to publish her novel *Gone With The Wind*. It sells 30 million copies.

"The girl doesn't, it seems to me, have a special perception or feeling which would lift that book above the 'curiosity' level." Perhaps the most misguided literary critique in history. With a further 15 rejections, there remained little hope her personal thoughts would see the light of day. Eventually, Doubleday brings the translation to the world, and *The Diary of Anne Frank* sells 25 million.

Thor Heyerdahl believes his book *Kon-Tiki: Across The Pacific* is unique. 20 publishers disagree. The 21st takes it on and sells 20 million: one million for each rejection.

"Unsaleable and unpublishable." Publisher on Ayn Rand's *The Fountainhead*. Random House takes a chance on it. It sells 7 million copies in the US alone.

To deal with publisher rejections, Hugh Prather decides to write a book about them in his early struggles and *Notes To Myself* sells 5 million.

30 publishers tell Laurence Peter that his book *The Peter Principle* will never sell. In 1969, a mere 18 months later it is a number #1 best-seller.

So how many of these great works wouldn't have seen the light of day were it not for the refusal of the authors to throw in the towel? It took hard work and an unfailing belief in the worthiness of their words and, eventually, success came.

Your level of commitment to the sharing of your message with the world via your book and other mediums will be the primary determinant of your success. Just don't become too discouraged if that success doesn't happen overnight.

Mistake #5

No Understanding of the Various Publishing Models

Book publishing has changed more in the last ten years then it did in all the previous years since Johannes Gutenberg invented the printing press back in 1450. Just a few short years ago traditional publishers ruled the book world and all potential authors had to live within the framework that the traditional publishers had created.

That traditional publishing world has, however, been flipped on its ear and these days authors have more publishing options then they have ever had. Each option has its own benefits and its own weaknesses so it is important for you, as an author, to have a full understanding of the various publishing models and the pros and cons associated with each so you can determine which publishing model best fits your needs.

---

*"There are several publishing models from which
you can choose. Which one is right for you is
something only you yourself can determine"*

Let's start by defining what are widely viewed as the major publishing models today. These are:

#1 Traditional publishing
#2 Self-publishing
#3 Vanity publishing
#4 Hybrid publishing

Traditional Publishing

Historically, a traditional book publishing company purchases the rights to an author's manuscript. Purchase of those rights is how book publishers have traditionally acquired new books. Usually, a literary agent, representing you as the author, negotiates the deal with the book publisher and, in return, gets a percentage of any monies earned from the sale of your book.

Part of the arrangement may include payment of an advance by the book publisher to the author to secure the book deal. In return, the author, working with that publisher's in-house editor, is expected to finish writing the book in an allotted time—which can often be years away. The advance is then deducted by the book publisher from any royalties the author receives from the sale of the book.

Royalties are usually based on a mutually agreed upon percentage of sales. You, as the author, do not receive any royalties until the advance has been paid back in full. The book publisher budgets funds to promote and market the book with this amount varying widely depending on the publisher's perception of the marketability of your book.

You are often strongly encouraged to hire a book publicist and to work aggressively to promote your own book. The book publisher has the final say on every aspect of your book, from editorial content to cover design to the number of books in the first printing. The book publisher alone makes the determination, based on declining sales, as to when they will allow your book to go out of print—this could be as short as a year or even less.

As an author you need to be aware of this, because some traditional publishers are putting their out of stock or back-list titles into commercial print-on-demand systems so the book isn't technically out of print and the book's rights will never revert back to you as the author.

Each day, agents and book publishers receive a staggering number of inquiries and manuscripts. Ultimately, less than 1% of authors seeking to be published traditionally are successful. Thousands of authors and their books are rejected daily.

Self-Publishing

Self-publishing is the publication of any book by the author of the book, without the involvement of an established third-party publisher. A self-published physical book is said to be privately printed. If you self-publish, you as the author are responsible and in control of entire process including:

- the design of your book cover
- layout of your book interior
- pricing of your book
- distribution of your book
- marketing of your book
- public relations for your book

You, as the author, can do all these things yourself or outsource all or part of the process to companies that offer these various services.

The key distinguishing characteristic of self-publishing is that you have decided to publish your book independent of a publishing house. In the past, self-published authors had to spend considerable amounts of money preparing a book for publication, and to purchase bulk copies of their title and find a place to store them.

Print-on-demand and ebook technologies have changed the game entirely. Now you can access global distribution channels like Amazon. com, can have a book printed or digitally delivered—virtually world-wide—only when an order has been placed.

2008 was the first year that more books were self-published than were published traditionally. The percentage of books self-published has continued to increase ever since. There is no doubt that self-publishing will continue to play a key role in the publishing world of tomorrow.

Vanity Publishing

A vanity publisher is a term describing a type of publishing house where you, as the author, pay to have your book published. The term actually appeared in mainstream U.S. publications as early as 1941. Traditional publishers derive their profit from sales of your book to the general public. Therefore, they must be cautious and deliberate in choosing to publish works that will sell, particularly as they must recoup their investment in the book.

Because vanity presses are not selective, publication by a vanity press is typically not seen as conferring the same recognition or prestige as traditional publishing. Vanity presses do offer more independence for the author than does the mainstream publishing industry. However, their fees can be higher than the fees normally charged for similar printing services, and sometimes restrictive contracts are required.

While a traditional publisher's intended market is the general public, a vanity publisher's intended market is the author and a very small number of interested members of the general public. In some cases, authors of a book that is vanity published will buy a substantial number of copies of their book, so that they can give it away as a promotional tool.

Hybrid Publishing

Though the models vary, three features distinguish some of the most successful hybrid publishers from traditional publishing and self-publishing.

#1—No Large Advances—While some hybrid publishers may offer small advances they don't pay advances on the scale of a large traditional publisher. This allows these publishers to price their books more aggressively to gain market share without losing money. In return, authors earn higher royalties which are usually paid monthly.

On the flip side, most hybrid publishers don't charge their authors to publish. This gives them a marketable advantage against self-publishing or vanity publishing where you, the author pay the upfront costs.

#2—Smaller Staffs—Many hybrid publishers operate with very few salaried employees. This low cost structure and the entrepreneurial structure of hybrid publishers gives them another important advantage: agility. In fact, their most important tool may be their ability to mimic self-publishers in speed to market while bringing considerably greater resources to bear:

#3—Agile Marketing—The book market operates like most other consumer goods markets. New segments emerge, expand and then sometimes implode. Traditional large publishers have long struggled to exploit growing market segments because their product development cycle operates in slow motion. Even when a manuscript is finished it sometimes takes a year or more to publish the book. Hybrid publishers, in contrast, turn out books dramatically quicker.

In the hands of a smart book marketer, this agility pays big dividends. Hybrid publishers may have another advantage, though, because not only are they relatively speedy, but they also tend to attract like-minded authors. They draw in self-published authors looking to expand their footprint and they also appeal to traditional authors looking for more control and higher royalties who are already savvy in marketing books.

In summary, there are obviously several publishing models from which you can choose. Which one is right for you is something only you yourself can determine.

Lack of Perception of Perceived Value in Information Marketing

At its core, a book is simply an information product. You have information you want to share with an audience and your book is the vehicle by which you wish to share that information. As an information product, your marketing efforts for your book make you also what's known in the industry as an information marketer.

Many authors are so focused on their book that they neglect to look at their overall world of information marketing. Why is that so important? In the information marketing world there is a concept known as "perceived value" that can have a dramatic impact on how you choose to "package" your information products like your book.

When you go into a bookstore what do you expect to pay for a book? $12.95 to $17.95 roughly for a softcover book and maybe $19.95

to $29.95 for a hardcover book. That's what we've been trained our entire lives that a book is worth.

Yet, you can take the exact same information that is in your book and "package" it differently and sell that same information for more money. Maybe instead of doing a traditional 5-1/2" x 8-1/2" softcover book you take your pages and you format them for 8-1/2" x 11" sheets and then 3-hole punch them and insert them into a 3-ring binder with your own custom graphics.

Now, you can possibly sell that exact same content, just packaged differently, for maybe $27 to $47. Let's repeat that—the content is exactly the same but by packaging it differently you are able to command a higher price point.

"By packaging your information differently
you can command higher prices"

Here's something else to consider. There are four primary learning modalities by which people prefer to consume information. Some people are readers and your book is perfect for them. But others are auditory learners and would prefer to listen to your information vs. reading it. Others still are more visual and would prefer to watch something while, finally, some people are more hands on and prefer live events where they can get experiential learning.

You can take your book and simply add an audio version of the same content and sell it as a bundled product. Not only do you have a wider audience you might appeal to because your product is addressing more than one learning modality, you also have a product with higher perceived value. Now maybe you can charge $47 - $97 for the same content that's simply packaged a bit differently.

Add a video component in DVD format or some checklists or other materials that are more of a hands-on nature and you have the makings of a home study course. Depending upon your market, we've seen home study courses sell anywhere from $97 up to $1997. As a general rule, the more learning modalities you incorporate into an information product the wider audience you'll possibly appeal to and the higher price you'll be able to charge.

Why such a variation in price? A lot of it has to do with what we call "hard" topics and "soft" topics in the information marketing world. A hard topic is usually something about making money, such as "How to Make Money in Real Estate," or "How to Make Money in the Stock Market." Typically, hard topics will command a higher price point in the market than what we call "soft" topics.

A soft topic is something like "How to Improve Your Relationship with Your Spouse" or "How to Be a Better You."

An aspect to the perceived value of your information product is undoubtedly the actual packaging. Let's say you decide to sell your book in audiobook format so you record the audio and burn it to CD. You can get up to about 80 minutes of audio on a single CD and, depending on how quickly one reads, an hour of audio is about 35 written pages.

So if you have a 200 page book you've got approximately 6 hours of audio content. With a maximum capacity of 80 minutes per disc your book would require 5 regular CDs to deliver to the end customer. If you're selling this product for $25 or more you better package it in a multi-disc CD case or multi-disc DVD style case so the packaging is in line with what one would expect if they're shelling out $25 of their money to buy your product.

Put those 5 CDs into paper sleeves, bundle it together with a rubber band and drop it in the mail and you're likely to have some unhappy customers. Why? Because your packaging is inconsistent with what one would expect to receive if they're spending $25 for your product. Your packaging falls short of expectations.

As a general rule, the price at which you're selling an information product should be a 10:1 markup over your hard costs to produce your product and get it in the hands of your customer. Some people say 8:1 and others 12:1 so we'll just split it down the middle. That means you may not, in some situations, be able to go as high end on your packaging as you might want.

Let's say you're selling a product that, for whatever reason, the market has said they're not willing to pay any more than $50. That means you need to figure out how you can package your product for about $5 to make the numbers work long term for you. Now, we're not saying that if you have a lead generation product (such as a book) that gets them into your funnel and you can sell them higher priced items on the back end that you can't do that. Just be sure you know your conversion numbers first.

Perceived value, the 10:1 rule of information marketing and hard vs. soft topics are all concepts involved in information marketing that you do need to understand. Just bear in mind when you're writing your book that there may be better ways to deliver your content than simply with a book. Should you have a book? Absolutely. But you should also have things beyond the book that you can offer your audience.

> Want to learn more about information marketing?
> Get your free subscription to the *Info Marketers Newsletter*
> at InfoMarketersNewsletter.com

Mistake #7

Trying to Do Too Many Products at the Same Time

I t's a quandary that many authors face. You know you need to get your book finished but at the same time you also know you need to have back end products in place when you launch your book. That means other products and/or services will need to be fully developed and in place prior to the release of your book. That is, of course, if your book is functioning as a lead generation device as we discussed earlier in the book.

We realize that so many authors are trying to get their book written as they continue to work a full-time job. That job may or may not be as an information marketer. So the writing of your book is probably just one of many products you have that are in various stages of development or is another task you need to accomplish in addition to your regular job.

"Beware the multiple project trap"

So let's call the writing of your book your "Project A". And, for argument's sake let's say if you applied full-time effort to the writing of your book you could do it in three months. But, in addition to your book, you are also working on three other projects that may or may not be related to your book. If you applied full-time effort to any of those other three projects, each one of them could be completed and out to market within just three months.

These other three projects we'll call "Project B", "Project C" and "Project D." Now, if you're like most authors and information marketers your ability to really focus on a single project and see it through to completion is a major challenge. Sound like you? So you jump from Project A to Project B and then to C and back to A and then to D and then over to B and, well you get the idea. On top of this the proverbial "Shiny Object Syndrome" comes into play and you find yourself being distracted by other opportunities that seem too good to pass up. So soon Projects A, B, C and D are joined by Projects E and F. And maybe even G, H and I.

Each of your projects could be a potential moneymaker so you decide that you can't let any of them go. So you continue to jump from project to project to project to project. You're making some progress on a few fronts but here's the problem. If it takes you three months of focused effort to finish just one project, whether it's the writing of your book or something else, as soon as that project is completed you now have the ability to take the resulting product and put it out to market. Now you can begin to generate some revenue from it.

If you're continually project jumping, instead of having a product completed and generating revenue for you after three months you have six or more projects that are all works in process. If it takes three months to complete each project when full-time effort is applied then you will not have any product fully completed and in revenue generation mode for you until 18 months down the road if you are working on six projects contiguously.

Obviously, only you can decide how you're going to allocate your time. Ideally, if the completion of your book is the most important thing to you then the majority of your project time should be invested in getting your book completed. Your back end product that your book will drive people to should be your Project B and completion of it shouldn't lag too far behind the completion of your book so you can get your book launched properly.

Some authors actually get so excited about getting their book done that they launch the book without having their back end product(s) in place. Big mistake!

Let's face it—we all have the same amount of time to work with every day. 24 hours. 1,440 minutes. 86,400 seconds. How will you spend yours? You definitely need to do what we call "Prioritize to Maximize" to get the greatest overall results. Project jumping and the Shiny Object Syndrome will be challenges that you're undoubtedly going to face. How will you overcome those challenges?

Time management is one of the least sexy topics that exist today. Nothing sounds as boring. Yet, your ability to manage your time effectively will dramatically impact how successful you are as an author. There are lots of time management systems out there but we highly recommend, as a starting point if you need help in this area, reading David Allen's "*Getting Things Done.*"

David points out that daily to-do lists don't work and offers a system to handle all the "stuff" that comes into your world every day in a way that helps you keep focused on the more important activities such as writing your book. His setting up your "buckets" and action planning sections are very helpful as well as his four criteria model for choosing actions in the moment.

His four criteria model is covered extensively in chapter 9 of his book and outlines those criteria on which your action choices must be based—context, time available, energy available and priority. Having yourself and your workspace organized will pay big dividends. How much time do you currently waste trying to find things you know you stuck somewhere?

Is anything about time management easy? No, not really. But if you simply just fly by the seat of your pants every day in terms of what you're going to focus your energies on you won't be nearly as effective or as efficient as you could be. And, with the limited hours available to you being both effective and efficient are very important factors to your on-going success as an author.

So Mr. or Ms. Author, when you're evaluating all of the projects on your plate—your Project A and your Project B and your Project C and so on—how will your "Prioritize to Maximize"?

Section 2

THE BUSINESS
OF YOUR BOOK

Mistake #8

Overproducing on an Initial Book Launch to Lower Per Unit Cost

We've seen it time and time again, especially with new authors getting a book published for the first time. They become so consumed with getting the lowest possible unit cost on the printing of their new book they order 5000 copies right out of the gate. So instead of paying $3.98 or $4.98 per book they get the unit price down to $2.98. Hooray, they saved a dollar or two per copy.

What happens next? 100 cases of books weighing 40 pounds or more each arrives at their home. They get stacked in the corner of the bedroom or in the garage, and there they sit, month after month after month. Sure, a few cases may be opened and some books shipped, but you're constantly stepping over and around boxes and cursing yourself for ordering so many books. You've tied up potentially thousands of dollars in inventory that you hope you can sell someday. And, in many cases, someday never comes. But hey, you saved $1 or $2 per book.

"Unless you have a proven track record and can accurately predict how many books you can sell, you're better off spending more per unit and having a lower quantity produced initially"

Unless you have a proven track record and can accurately predict how many books you can sell, you're better off spending more per unit and having a lower quantity produced initially. Print on demand services such as Create Space, 48 Hour Books, or Lulu can be invaluable until you've got your marketing channels fully working and generating regular sales for you. You can conceivably tie up tens of thousands of dollars in production for books you hope you can sell — all because it saved you some money on the up front printing cost per book.

And, if you're working with a fulfillment service you'll end up giving a lot of your "savings" back in storage charges for all your pallets of books. Fulfillment house storage charges can vary widely, but let's be conservative and say it costs you $15 to store a pallet at their facility each month. If you have 5000 books printed and shipped to your fulfillment house then, depending upon the size of your book, you might have 7 pallets being stored. At $15 per pallet that's $105 out of your pocket each and every month. 7 pallets sitting for a year at a fulfillment house is $1260 in direct costs to you. So much for the money you saved on the per copy costs. You've given all or most of it back in the storage charges.

But what do you do if you sell more product than you expected? In these print-on-demand days in the publishing world it's really not so much of an issue. In just a few days you can have more books printed. But you do need to have a plan in place to deal with your customers in the event your book launch is more successful than you anticipated. A nice problem to have but one that you must be prepared to deal with.

Let's say you have 500 copies of your book on hand, whether it's at your house and you're doing your own order shipping or whether you're working with a fulfillment house such as Bret and Bryan's own Speaker Fulfillment Services. If you do a book launch and sell 800 units you've created a potential problem you'll have to deal with to keep your customers happy.

It's primarily a matter of managing customer expectations. If you keep your customers informed about the status of things proactively, you can significantly reduce any possible negatives that can result from having customers in a back order scenario. Maybe you can give them the ebook version of your book to get started with until the physical copy arrives in the mail.

It is best to under promise and over deliver in most cases. If you tell your customers that their book will ship in three days and you ship it in five days than you're a bum. You didn't live up to what you had promised. But if you promise three days and ship it in one or two than you're a hero—you over delivered. It really is all about communication and managing customer expectations.

If you're working with a fulfillment house their system should be able to generate an email to your customer notifying them when their book order has shipped out the door, including tracking information if appropriate.

> For more information on Bret and Bryan's fulfillment services
> visit SpeakerFulfillmentServices.com

When you go beyond your book and get into the production of home study courses and higher ticket items the minimization of your initial risk becomes even more important. Now, instead of talking about $2.98 or $3.98 to print a book and trying to save a buck or two you can be talking about $25 or $35 or $50 or $100 or more to produce your product depending on what all components make up that product.

So, your initial out of pocket cost to produce some larger quantity of your home study course can be really significant and until you're sure your marketing is working well you're far better off doing a smaller quantity run and paying a higher cost per unit.

Book printing costs are very quantity sensitive. A large portion of the cost is in what they call the setup and, obviously, the greater number of units you can amortize that setup cost across the lower your per unit cost will be per book. Until you are absolutely, positively sure you're able to sell all you are going to get printed, don't get seduced by those lower per unit costs. We have a client who produced a beautiful full color cookbook and had 15 pallets of books shipped to our warehouse. Now, three years later 15 pallets of books still sit in our warehouse. A very painful and expensive lesson.

Should you have high expectations? Of course. We all want to have the greatest of success with our publishing efforts. But, as all businesses do, you need to carefully watch your cash flow and be aware of how much money you have tied up in inventory. Remember, your book is a business.

Not Understanding the Lifetime Value of a Reader

In marketing there is an important concept called Lifetime Customer Value (LCV). If you don't know this number then you don't know how much you can afford to spend to acquire a customer. You're totally shooting in the dark with your marketing when you have no idea of what marketing channels are working for you and what the cost of acquiring a new customer is and what that customer is worth to you over their lifetime.

As a book marketer insert the word "reader" in place of customer. And ask yourself the question "What is my Lifetime Reader Value?"

We first learned about the concept of lifetime customer value from marketing legend Jay Abraham way back in the mid-1990s. This critical concept can be applied to any type of business, including the business of your book.

The basic calculation of your Lifetime Customer Value is a simple one. Just divide your revenue over time by the number of customers who generated that revenue. That gives you the average lifetime value of a customer to you. You can use that figure to determine how much you can afford to spend to acquire a new customer.

Now, we think it is more important to think of this in terms of the profitability of a customer rather than just the pure gross sales revenue. If you have hard costs associated with making a sale those should be taken into account before deciding the justifiable new customer acquisition cost you can afford to absorb. Those hard costs could include printing and delivery costs of your book.

We discussed much earlier in this book that the real value of your book lies in the value of the back end products and services that you'll be able to sell to your book readers. Maybe it's a home study course or a maybe it's a membership site or maybe it's a live event. It doesn't matter what it is.

"How much is each reader worth to you over their lifetime?"

They key here is to determine how much, on average, each person you get to read your book is worth to you over their lifetime.

Let's say, for example, that you have a book you sell for $15 off your website and 1000 people have bought your book. Then let's say you have a home study course that you sell for $500 that your book drives people to. Of those 1000 readers, let's say 5% take the next step and purchase your home study course. That means 50 people purchase your higher level product.

That means your total revenue is ($15 x 1000) + ($500 x 50) = $40,000. That means the average Lifetime Reader Value is $40,000 / 1000 = $40 per reader. So everyone you got to read your $15 book was, in reality, worth $40 to you. Make sense?

Here's another example for illustrative purposes. Let's say your back end product that your book is driving people to is a membership site that sells for $97 per month. Assume you acquire the same 1000 readers as in the previous example. So you're still grossing $15,000 in book sales as a starting point.

But in your membership site you find that, on average, your reader who joins stays with you for six months. That means they are paying you an additional $97 x 6 = $582 on top of that $15 book purchase.

In this scenario your lifetime reader value, assuming the same 5% conversion rate, is now ($15 x 1000) + ($582 x 50) = $44,100. So the value of your average reader is now $44.10 each.

Now, for the purposes of these examples, to keep things simple, we did not factor in the hard costs of book printing and fulfillment which you'll need to do when you go to run your numbers.

You should also remember to segregate your customer list in different ways as part of your analysis process. Customers who participate in a continuity program of yours may have greater value than others. Or people that attend live events may be of greater value.

You should also look at your various lead generation sources. You may find that one particular marketing channel generates far more valuable customers to you than another. Or you might find certain socio-economic groups, or countries, or sex, or ethnic group might generate higher value customers.

Large organizations have been built off of literally giving books away. We recommend you study Brendon Burchard or T. Harv Eker for example. T. Harv Eker built his large training organization Peak Potentials by giving away tickets to a live event of his right within his book *Secrets of the Millionaire Mind*. Harv recognized the money was in the back end and not in the book itself.

Similarly, Brendon Burchard used his book *The Millionaire Messenger* as a front end product to his higher priced membership community and to his live Experts Academy events. He could do this because he knew his numbers. He knew the value of each reader to him over their lifetime if he could just get them to read his book. So he gave away a lot of books.

Now, we certainly do not recommend that you immediately start giving books away. This is especially true if you don't know your back end conversion numbers. That's a dangerous game to play until you have your marketing channels working real well and you have a firm grasp of your ability to convert readers into higher end products and services.

We also recognize when you're just starting out you don't have a track record. You have no history. So that's why you need to put your tracking mechanisms in place early in the game to start gathering your data so you can determine what these numbers are. It doesn't happen overnight. But, over time, the data you collect about the value of your readers will pay massive dividends. When you know how much you can afford to spend to acquire a reader it is a total game changer for your marketing efforts.

You should know your Lifetime Reader Value. It's critical to your long-term success.

You Don't Know Your Numbers

What numbers are we talking about? All sorts of numbers! Numbers like:

- How much do you make per book sold if you go with a traditional publisher?
- How much do you make per book sold if you self-publish?
- How much will it cost to print your book?
- How much does it cost to ship a book?
- How much does it cost to store books?
- How much does it cost to accept credit card orders?

Understanding the math behind the book publishing business is an important factor in your achieving success as an author. When you don't know your numbers you end up making uninformed and, in many cases, poor decisions. All the numbers above don't necessarily directly relate to each other but all can bite you in the butt if you don't know them.

Let's take a look at each of these in a little detail.

How much do you make per book sold if you go with a traditional publisher?

As an author there are three ways you can make money directly from your book:

1. An advance from the publisher
2. Royalties off your book sales
3. Reselling your book yourself

In most cases, if you're writing your first book, you're probably not going to receive an advance from a traditional publisher. If you do receive an advance, the typical range is somewhere between $4,000 and $10,000. It's important to remember that this is an advance, so you have to pay that money back to the publisher.

Typically publishers offer you a contract where you get 10-15% royalties of each sale. You'll need to pay attention as to whether that rate is based on the list price of your book (gross royalties) or whether that rate is based off the amount of profit they make off your book (net royalties). Usually, the net amount runs about 50% of the list price of your book's price.

So, let's look at an example. Let's say your book has a list price of $20.00. If your contract states you'll receive 10% royalties off list, then you'll get $2.00. If you're receiving 10% of net profits, you'll receive around $1.00 per book. Most publishers prefer to offer net royalties.

Also, it's likely you can get a higher royalty rate for ebooks and you may also be offered a higher royalty rate as the sales of your book go up. You should be prepared to ask a publisher for both.

Let's do some quick math here. Let's say you get a $4,000 advance for your book and you get 10% royalties net profit, and the book's list price is $20.00. That means you are making $1.00 per book, and that you will need to sell 4,000 copies of your book just to break even. The averages say you will never make a penny from royalties off sales of your book, as the average non-fiction book sells only about 250 copies a year and just about 3,000 over its lifetime.

All the more reason why you need to recognize your book should be your front end product to get you in the door and the real money will be made on the back end.

How much do you make per book if you self-publish?

If you self-publish your book and sell a copy yourself then you're making whatever the price you sold your book for less your hard costs to have your book printed. So if you sell that book for $20 and it costs you $4 to print it your net is $16 per copy. In reality, that net of $16 is a contribution to overhead as all of your other costs as an author—advertising and marketing, bookkeeping, travel, etc. will have to be accounted for.

Of course, you'll have all these same costs to account for if you go with a traditional publisher. So, why wouldn't everyone automatically chose the self-published route where you are looking at $16 vs. $1 per book sold? Two factors—#1 Self-publishing requires you to pretty much do most everything yourself and #2 Distribution—getting it can be pretty much impossible for self-published authors.

How much will it cost to print your book?

Many factors go into determining the printing costs for a book. These include:

- Number of pages
- Trim size of book (5-1/2 x 8, 6 x 9, etc.)
- Black and white print or color interior
- Paper type selected
- Binding method
- Quantity to be printed

Of these perhaps the quantity is the biggest driving factor. So much of the cost of a printing job is in the setup of the presses. The more copies of a book you can spread those setup costs across, the lower the per unit cost, as the quantity printed increases.

"The more copies of a book you can spread your printing setup costs across, the lower your per unit cost."

If you go the print-on-demand route where your book may be getting printed a single unit at a time through services like CreateSpace, Lulu, or 48 Hour Books then you're usually looking at a per unit cost of somewhere between $4.50 and $5.50 per copy. This is a rough guideline as some of the other factors we mentioned can also come into play and affect your per unit cost.

If you don't go with a print-on-demand book printer then you might have anywhere from a couple hundred to a few thousand books printed at a time. Of course you'll have to figure out how you're going to store them and there are costs associated with that. But the book printing cost itself can range anywhere from around $1 per copy up to $5 to $6 or more each depending on all the variables mentioned before.

How much does it cost to ship a book?

Most book orders these days seem to ship via the United States Postal Service's media mail category.

With the typical softcover book these days weighing under a pound you can mail a book anywhere in the U.S. for, as of the time this book was written, $2.92. If it's over a pound but less than two pounds the rate goes to $3.40. Check USPS.gov for current rates. Keep in mind this is the actual shipping cost and if you're using a fulfillment house to ship your book orders you will have a fulfillment charge in addition to the postage costs you'll need to account for.

Larger orders such as multiple book orders to distributors or Amazon warehouses usually also ship via media mail, as it's considerably less expensive than carriers like UPS or FedEx. Remember that paper is heavy and the weight can start to add up in a hurry if you're shipping very many copies of a book anywhere. Even with media mail you're going to spend somewhere north of $7 to ship a 10 lb. package, which might be anywhere from 5-10 copies of your book. Add on a corresponding amount for each additional 10 pounds being shipped.

Keep in mind also that if you're using a third party fulfillment house to ship your book orders in addition to the actual shipping cost there will likely be a fulfillment fee that you'll need to calculate into your total overall costs.

How much does it cost to store books?

This can vary from one fulfillment house to the next so be sure to do your own due diligence if you're considering a fulfillment house to handle your book orders. Bret and Bryan's company, Speaker Fulfillment Services (SpeakerFulfillmentServices.com) charges $15 per pallet per month for storage of books. A typical pallet when stacked mesures about 40" x 40" x 40" and the number of books that can be stored on a pallet varies from a few hundred to a couple thousand or so depending upon the size of the book.

How much does it cost to accept credit card orders?

There will come a time, probably sooner rather than later where you'll want to sell your book via your own website. That means you'll probably need to accept credit cards at some point in time. It's fine to begin with just PayPal for orders on your site, and PayPal will usually take 2.9% of the sales amount plus 30 cents per transaction as their cut.

Eventually, however you'll want to accept credit cards (Visa, MasterCard, American Express, Discover), as it will typically increase your sales by accepting more payment methods. But you'll need to decide when that time is right for you. A merchant account provider that sets you up with the ability to accept credit cards has a cost associated with it every month whether or not you're getting any sales. So you need to make sure you're going to have the sales level to justify the out-of-pocket costs you'll be facing.

On average you're going to give up about 2.3% of the sale plus a 25-cent transaction fee when you accept a credit card payment. But your costs just to have the account usually amount to around $50 per month just for having the account.

> Need a Merchant Account?
> Check out InfoMarketingMerchantAccount.com

Are these all the costs you'll need to think about as an author? Of course not. But we wanted to stimulate your thinking about the math and the associated economic realities you'll face as an author.

Not Knowing How Bookstores Really Work

There is a certain romance to the notion of having your book in bookstores. Almost nothing is as exciting for an author as to be browsing their local Barnes and Noble or Books-a-Million or other independent bookstore and coming across their title on the shelf.

With the number of actual physical bookstores shrinking dramatically you've first got to question how important as an author is it for you to be found in a bookstore? Certainly not as important as it once was with Amazon ruling the book-selling world now but, in our opinion, it is still something that is worthwhile if you can make it happen.

Many authors have a significant misunderstanding about how these chain bookstores and how their local independent bookstore make decisions on which books they're going to place on their shelves. How do people get their book onto the shelves of a brick and mortar bookstore?

"It isn't easy to get your book stocked in a bookstore"

Suffice it to say, it isn't easy to get your book stocked in a bookstore. With somewhere between two and three million new books entering the marketplace every year there is no way in the world that all of those titles are going to get bookstore space.

In the corporate chain stores like Barnes and Noble and Books-a-Million the decision to stock books is not made at a store level. It's made by a buyer who works in the corporate office for these bookstore chains. These buyers only deal with the publisher and you, as an author, should not contact them directly. In reality, each bookstore chain will have several buyers, each of who will specialize in a particular genre of book.

The corporate buyers will take several different things into consideration when making the decision whether to add a book to their stores' stock. Things such as:

- Has this author published previously?
- If yes, how did their previous books sell?
- How well have related books sold in their stores?
- Are they already well stocked with books in the same niche?

Naturally, books from celebrities or from authors who have had bestsellers previously go to the top of their list. If a store already has 25 titles about relationships in their store they probably aren't interested much in a 26th title.

Keep in mind also that some publishers also pay for product placement in stores. The prime real estate, usually near the front of a store, is already spoken for. So, even if you're able to get your book into a store don't expect it to be front and center.

The actual store managers usually don't have much say about which books are stocked in their store. They do have the ability to order books for book signings and might stock a few selected titles for their "local interest" section, but that's about all.

As an author you can call your local chain bookstore and ask to participate in a book signing. If the event goes well and their customers continue to request your book the store manager may locally stock the book in their "local interest" section. If their corporate buyer then notices growing customer demand for a particular title they might eventually decide to stock that title in other stores.

Books handled by a distributor have a distinct advantage over books which are only available directly from the publisher. Book buyers want books at a discount and they want to be able to return the books if they don't sell. This usually disqualifies any self-published title.

Local independent bookstores are a different beast. These "mom and pops" usually make the decision to stock a title right in the store. It might come by the storeowner or manager or with some input from the store's employees. They definitely have more latitude to stock books from local authors.

You can contact the managers of these stores directly. You show them your book and, if they think it will sell, they'll stock it. They may order the book directly from a distributor or they might have you leave a few copies that they'll sell on a consignment basis. If it sells well, they'll order more. If you're going to provide some books to a local bookstore on a consignment basis, meaning they'll pay you when a book sells and not in advance, be sure to protect yourself with some type of written agreement. The standard discount off list price that bookstores expect is 40%. Some retail or specialty shops will want 50%.

For a link to a handy sample consignment agreement
visit our resources page at
MistakesAuthorsMake.com/resources

The airport bookstore is another avenue of opportunity if your book is appropriate.

There are two major players in the airport bookstore world. These are Hudson News, which is based in New Jersey (online at HudsonGroup.com) and the Paradies Shops, which is Georgia based (online at TheParadiesShops.com). These are the 800-pound gorillas in airport book sales.

Next time you're traveling spend some time in the airport bookstore and see what types of books they're carrying. If the manager is available ask what types of books are moving best for them. Tell them you're thinking about marketing your book to Hudson News or The Paradies Shops and see if they feel your book would move in their store.

Will all bookstores go the way of the dinosaur at some point in time? Who really knows for sure. But for now they're still a viable way to sell books and your understanding of how they function will help. Remember, if you're working with a traditional publisher they should be working to get your book sold to the corporate buyers as a part of the services they're providing to you. If you're self-publishing it's considerably more challenging and the entire burden will fall on your shoulders.

You should certainly get to know your local bookstore owners and managers. They can be great sources of information that might help you in your on-going marketing efforts.

Trying to Wear Too Many Hats

et's face it—there are a lot of steps involved in bringing a new book to market. You've got the writing, the proofreading, the cover design, the interior layout, typesetting and the copy editing. And all that's even before the book is finished and available for sale.

We recognize that many first time authors are operating with limited funding and, as a result, may need to handle certain tasks themselves that, in an ideal world, would be handled by others. We get it. We've been there ourselves.

So what's your time worth? $10, $20, $50 per hour? More?

But, in a sense, it comes down to what do you value your time at? $10 per hour? $20? $50, $100, $500 or more? We all have the same amount of time available to us every day. If you value your time highly, and you should, then any time you're spending doing $10 per hour tasks will limit the growth of your business.

You need to also ask yourself if you are qualified to wear a particular hat. If you are a terrible speller or your grammar sucks then you're just kidding yourself if you want to put the proofreader hat on. That's a quick route to development of a crappy book.

So what are the various "hats" one must wear to bring a book to market and what are the responsibilities that go with that hat?

Author—We already talked in chapter 1 about the difference between being the writer and being the author of the book. Are you going to be the one to put the words to paper in some way or are you going to call upon someone else to do it on your behalf? Obviously, this is the first critical hat that you need to decide if you're going to wear or not.

Copy Editor—Copy editing is the work that an editor does to improve the formatting, style, and accuracy of text. Unlike general editing, copy editing might not involve changing the content of the text. Copy editing is done before proofreading, the latter of which is the last step in the editorial cycle.

Proofreader—In addition to looking for obvious typos in your book, a proofreader makes sure your grammar usage is appropriate. It is a common fallacy that proofreading is the same as editing. The term *proofreading* is sometimes used to refer to copy editing, and vice versa. Although there is necessarily some overlap, proofreaders usually lack any real editorial or managerial authority: their only available course of action is to raise queries with editors or authors. Thus proofreading and editing are fundamentally separate responsibilities.

Cover Designer—Studies have shown that a potential reader will glance at your front book cover for 8 seconds and your back cover for 15 seconds before deciding whether or not to buy your book. That's not a lot of time to make a good impression. That's why good cover design is so important to the success of a book. So a graphics designer with a great understanding of the elements of good cover design including font usage and the critical information to include on the front and back cover of your book is what you're looking for. Maybe that's you and maybe that's not you.

Interior Designer—The interior layout of your book is also an important consideration. Your book pages must be pleasing to the eye. The layout should invite your reader to keep reading. A successful interior design matches the book's subject matter and tone and appeals to your intended readers. Traditionally, design and typesetting are separate steps.

Your designer (probably not you) creates the design and your typesetter implements it. The designer selects the typeface, its size, and the leading; decides how to indicate section breaks and the various levels of headings and how to treat illustrations and other graphical elements, and designs the most appropriate format for tables and figures.

Typesetter—The typesetter takes your designer's specifications and applies them to your manuscript. He or she reviews each page for poor hyphenation, for large gaps between words, and for other issues that may affect a page's beauty and readability. During typesetting, any illustrations, photographs, or other artwork will need to be prepared and placed at the appropriate spot in the book.

Many times the interior designer for your book will also take on the typesetting responsibilities, although they are two separate processes.

Bottom line is that there are a lot of different hats that you might wear for even getting your book ready for market. How many of these functions you will perform yourself is a question that only you can answer. Whether you could or should is a different matter entirely.

I've often heard our good friend and outstanding marketer Alex Mandossian say at events something to the effect of "To have success in business you must put people on your team who 'play' at those things that you have to work at."

It's so true. If something isn't among your core strengths then you'll probably waste more time and money trying to do it yourself. You always have to consider your opportunity cost in anything you decide to undertake. The time you spend doing something yourself is time that you're not spending doing something that may be of greater value to you in the long term.

Whether the folks you add to your team are employees, virtual assistants, outside vendors or somebody else doesn't really matter. You need to view them as business "amplifiers" that can free up your time to focus on the more important things.

Business amplifiers can include things as well as people. Maybe there's a piece of software that can automate some task you manually do now that will free up your time.

Will there be trade-offs you'll need to make as an author? Of course there are. But your ability to manage your time and focus the majority of your efforts on those things that only you can do and are of the greatest value in building your business is critical for your on-going success.

Not Understanding the Differences Between a Distributor and a Wholesaler and a Fulfillment House

The book distribution system that exists today seems to have come from the dark ages. Today's retail bookstores like Barnes and Noble or Books-a-Million are nothing more than consignment shops. They don't own the books they're selling. And, if your book doesn't sell this season they'll just send it back and move on to different titles.

Many self-publishers these days seem to think that just by getting their book printed at Lightning Source gives them "distribution." Or they go to some author services company and buy "distribution packages" that really amount to nothing more than a listing in the Ingram catalog. By this standard, distribution is equal to no more than a catalog listing. Your book is simply made available for purchase.

This is actually closer to the definition of a wholesaler and not a true distributor. Even your small-press distributors will attempt to sell the books of the publishers they represent. The larger traditional publishers don't just have a listing in a catalog—they have a dedicated sales force. The reps for this sales force work to develop a long-term relationship with key booksellers.

Just to be sure we're on the same page let's define a book distributor and a wholesaler.

A book distributor makes its money by marketing and merchandising the book their publishers create. They take an overall percentage of the retail-selling price. Distributors rarely work with individuals because they need an on-going stream of new titles regularly published every season in order to make a profit.

A wholesaler is a large warehouse that holds and sells books when retailers or other booksellers ask for them. They make their income off of the difference between the price that they buy a book for and the price at which they sell it to a retailer.

The traditional publisher supports retailers with cooperative advertising and national advertising for its big books. Authors who are celebrities are made available for various bookseller events and in store promotions. The traditional publisher's marketing department coordinates with Promotion and Sales to try to maximize the book's potential.

What the big publishers are able to do is both push their books into the retailers where book buyers can buy them and pull the buyers into the store with their advertising and promotional efforts. But the reason the big publisher can sell so many books is this distribution apparatus.

This distribution system makes it difficult for most self-publishers, and dooms a good many of them. You can make it work to your advantage if you have a book with steady sales. In other words, you will probably need to go out and create the demand for the book, before any distributor will take you on.

If you have a book with steady but modest sales, you may have to build up your publishing company until you have a line of closely related books, each of which sells, before a distributor will agree to take you on. Even then, you will only have a part of the whole coordinated distribution-marketing-advertising-promotion system being used by big publishers.

As an author you need to be clear on how you're going to get your book into the hands of customers. And you need to understand distributors versus wholesalers and what each can do for you. Both charge 25-35% of revenue earned. Some figure this off list price and others off of actual revenue. In other words, what is earned after the wholesalers or bookstores take their discount.

If your book marketing plan is directed primarily at bookstores and libraries you might consider getting your book with a distributor. You need to start looking for one prior to taking your book to press. If your marketing plan is primarily aimed at areas other than the book trade (back of the room sales after speeches for example), then you should probably skip distributors and look at vending directly to wholesalers.

Some of the bigger distributors can get your book into B&N, Costco and other retail outlets. But you must be prepared to do a lot of marketing to support that effort, or your books will all come back. It's hard to get attention as a 1-2 book press or as a self-publisher. Distributors help you leverage your title by being part of a larger organization.

"Many bookstores won't order your book unless it is listed in the Ingram catalog"

Most distributors get you into Ingram. Many bookstores will simply not order a book unless it is listed with this company. But, as we mentioned earlier, in most cases this is nothing but a catalog listing. Necessary yes, but don't expect it to move a lot of books for you simply by just being listed.

An advantage distributors offer you is time. They warehouse, pick, pack, ship, accept returns, bill and send you the check. This leaves you time to market your book. A good distributor will work with you. They will help make sure there are enough books in the system for upcoming events and can provide you feedback when you try different marketing tactics.

A disadvantage of distributors is that most are exclusive, which means you have to let them sell your book to the trade. Many don't take kindly to you selling off your own website.

They do add to your cost per book and are one additional layer between you and your reader. They may do a little marketing but you have to drive the marketing efforts.

Wholesalers are a different story. The big players are Ingram, Baker & Taylor and Quality Books. They take orders from bookstores and libraries and then order from the distributor or directly from the publisher. They expect a 55% discount.

If you refuse to discount or only offer them a smaller discount like 20% your book will be classified as a special order item and these wholesalers won't stock it. Booksellers are historically fretful about ordering a book that is listed as a special order item. For some books and marketing plans, this isn't a problem. For a traditional market plan targeted to the book trade this is an invitation to fiscal disaster.

Getting your book into Baker & Taylor and/or Ingram will get you stocked on Amazon, and probably at the 20% off discount.

Ingram is the 800 lb. gorilla of wholesalers. Ingram doesn't accept books from publishers of less than 10 titles or whose income from Ingram is less than around $30k per year.) This makes life very hard for the new or struggling small press. Most bookstores won't bother with a book that isn't listed in Ingram.

Baker & Taylor is more receptive to small presses. Be aware that unless there is significant ordering of your book Baker & Taylor will not stock it. They'll list it in their database and order only when there is activity. They also reportedly have a hair-trigger returns program, which means your books may come back seemingly just after you sent them out.

An advantage of wholesalers is you lower your cost per book by cutting out the distributor. A disadvantage is if you start having some strong sales due to your marketing efforts you'll find you're spending more time shipping books than doing other, more important, activities. At some point you'll have to decide if you want to hand off the book shipping to a fulfillment company like Speaker Fulfillment Services.

> Need Book Fulfillment?
> Check out Bret and Bryan's Company –
> SpeakerFulfillmentServices.com

Fulfillment companies are typically not involved in the promotion of your book in any way. They are simply packing and shipping book orders to customers on your behalf. If you're selling books on your website you'll set up an integration between your shopping cart and your fulfillment company so that orders are automatically transmitted to your fulfillment company as you receive an order.

You'll pay a per book or per order charge in most cases along with the actual shipping costs for book fulfillment. Your fulfillment company should allow you to select which shipping method(s) you want to offer your customers and they should be equally able to handle shipments to parties other than end customers such as Amazon.

Book Distribution vs. Wholesaling vs. Fulfillment can be a confusing world. It is your job to understand the differences that exist in order to determine which model may work best for you. There's an extremely instructive example from Sea Hill Press about how the book distribution plan you choose can impact your profits we encourage you to read. You can find it in the "Additional Reading" section of our resources page at MistakesAuthorsMake.com/resources.

Not Using a Literary Agent When You Need One and Using One When You Don't

The path to authorship can be like a minefield, especially in the world of traditional publishing. But there are potential pitfalls with any publishing model you choose, from vanity publishing to self-publishing. For the first time author it can become very confusing very fast.

One of the trickiest questions you need to answer early in the game is do you need a literary agent or not? What is a literary agent? A literary agent is a person who represents writers and their written works to publishers, film producers, theatrical producers and film studios and assists in the sale and negotiates the deal on your behalf.

Literary agents most often represent novelists, screenwriters and non-fiction writers. They are paid a fixed percentage, which is typically twenty percent on foreign sales and ten to fifteen percent for domestic sales of the proceeds of sales they negotiate on your behalf.

The size of literary agencies can vary. Some are single agent agencies who may represent from ten to twelve authors. Others are large, with senior partners, sub-agents, specialists in areas like foreign rights or licensed merchandise tie-ins, and a client base numbering in the hundreds.

Most agencies, especially the smaller ones, will specialize to some extent. For example, they may represent authors who just write science fiction, or mainstream thrillers and mysteries, or children's books, or highly topical nonfiction.

"Legitimate literary agents do not charge reading or retainers or charge you their operating expenses"

Legitimate literary agents do not charge reading or retainers or charge you their operating expenses. They also will not place your book with a vanity press. Either of these practices should be considered a red flag that you're working with a less than reputable agent.

But when do you need a literary agent and when don't you need one? If you're looking to go with a traditional publisher then an agent can definitely be of benefit. Most of the larger publishing houses only accept submissions from agents—as an author you can't go to them directly.

If you, however, are opting to self-publish then you there is no valid reason for you to have an agent.

But how do you go about finding a literary agent? The typical way authors establish a relationship with a literary agent is through a process called querying. A query is an unsolicited proposal for representation, either for a finished work or unfinished work.

Various agents may request different elements in a query packet. Most agencies list their specific submission requirements on their website or in their listing in major directories. A query typically begins with a one to two page query letter explaining the purpose of your book and your writing qualifications. Sometimes a synopsis is requested as part of the query. Often, the author sends the first 3 chapters of their book.

If a written query is rejected, the response is sent in the self-addressed stamped envelope that you should include with your written query. Typically, the rejection is a form letter. And, while disappointing, the receipt of a rejection that is not a form letter or has hand-written comments is typically taken as a positive sign.

But, there are ways to establish a relationship with a literary agent that are a bit "warmer" then this cold calling via query letter process. One of the most popular is via writer's conferences. These events can be a great way to meet a potential agent although some authors seem to muck up the entire process. There is a certain etiquette you are expected to follow when attending these events and to smooth this process we're delighted to share this helpful article from Scott Hoffman of Folio Literary Management.

Writers' Conference Etiquette
By Scott Hoffman

Those of you who have read some of the articles I've had published on how to find an agent know that I'm not the world's biggest fan of trying to land an agent by sending blind query letters. Does it work on occasion? Sure. We've gotten some of our best clients that way. But there's something so... passive about the process.

There's some element of ceding control that I know that I wouldn't be comfortable with if I were in an author's position. To me, the whole process seems to evoke bad memories of high school, sitting by the phone, waiting for it to ring to see if you're going to have a date on Saturday night, when you should have just been out having a good time with your friends anyway.

Besides, what do you do if your preferred agent or agents aren't accepting unsolicited queries in the first place?

That's where writers' conferences come in.

As an unpublished author, attending a reputable, well-run writers' conference can be the first step to launching your brilliant professional writing career. But it can also be an intimidating, frustrating experience if you approach it the wrong way.

For agents, writers' conferences are a mixed bag. They can be very positive experiences, full of promising new talent—or they can be grueling experiences that leave us vowing never to volunteer our time ever, ever again.

Here are a few tips to ensure that you get the most out of your writers' conference experience.

1. Develop a plan for the conference ahead of time. There are as many different reasons to attend conferences as there are attendees. What you can get out of a conference, however, is often a function of where you are in the publishing process. If you're still in the process of writing your novel or putting together a proposal for your nonfiction book, the craft seminars at the conference are probably where you want to spend most of your time.

    Figure out which authors, editors, and agents are teaching, and attend the sessions that are taught by the people whose work you most respect. (It's been my experience that, regardless of the purported subject of the lecture, speakers are going to talk about what they're best at anyway—so rather than choosing which sessions to attend based on the title of the talk, I suggest you go to the sessions taught by the coolest people—the best agents, authors, and editors. Even if a workshop is on plotting in science fiction and you're writing romance, what you'll learn from a master like Orson Scott Card, say, is likely to make you a better writer.

If you've already got an agent you're happy with, or if you've sold a book, or are a published author, conferences can still be tremendously valuable. They're an opportunity to promote yourself and your work, make additional professional contacts, and learn what other successful authors have done to take their work to the next level.

The most important thing you can do at this stage—listen. Let the pros know you're a rookie who's past that first stage of the game, and ask each one for their one best tip on how to succeed in the business. You can sometimes learn as much as you would in a master class this way.

If you're at that stage where you've written a novel but are still looking for an agent, however—you're in luck. Conferences are tailor-made for people like you. Take the rest of the tips in this section to heart.

2. Ignore the one on one meetings. I know this is going to be controversial advice, but I'll stand by it. I don't like formal author-agent pitch sessions for a couple of reasons. First, most conferences schedule too many of them. If you're one of the agent's first pitches you might be in good shape. But if you're the agent's 30th pitch in two days, honestly, you would have been better off sending a query letter. As to pitching editors directly, unless you're writing romance or science fiction, they're probably just going to tell you to get an agent anyway.

    Here's an inside tip on how agents deal with conferences. Most agents are too polite to say "no" to your face. You can pitch them a book that they KNOW—100% KNOW– they would never in a million years sign up. But rather than deal with the pressure of rejecting you to your face, they'll say something like "Well, I don't know. For something like this it's all in the writing." They'll ask you to mail them the first three chapters and then they'll glance at them for about 5 seconds and then pass, politely, with their standard rejection letter.

Here's a statistic from experience: in the past three years, I've sold about ten books from people I met at conferences. Not ONE of those authors did I meet at a one on one pitch session. So, how did those authors get to me? After my workshop. In the elevator. In the bar after dinner. Basically, in normal, organic situations that aren't terribly forced like those awful one on one pitch sessions. In ways that proved to me that they would be effective advocates for their work once it hit the shelves.

3. Ignore what the conference organizers tell you to do. Conference organizers are going to get mad at me for this one. But I'm on your side here, so I'm going to give you the straight dope. I'd say about half of the conferences I've been to are not particularly well run. They try their best, but they're usually volunteers with jobs and lives and families and don't always know what to do to help your career prospects along. So, regardless of what the conference organizers tell you, there are a few things you should always have with you at a conference:

   • A memorized, one sentence explanation of what your book is about that's catchy and explanatory. "It's a literary retelling of the Noah's Ark story." "It's about a young Japanese-American man and woman who fall in love on the eve of World War II and are torn apart by the war." Practice this one in front of the mirror. I promise you an agent is going to ask you what your book is about when you're not expecting it. This is your chance to differentiate yourself.

- A one page synopsis of your novel (if you're writing fiction) or your completed, polished nonfiction proposal if you're writing nonfiction, and a one-page bio of yourself.
- The first three chapters of your novel, double-spaced.
- A copy of your manuscript—just in case.

Carry these with you at all times. Chances are nobody will ever ask for them—but if they do, bam. You have them. Don't ever try to foist them on agents or editors, but they'll be your secret weapon. And you'll be more confident knowing you have them if you need them.

4. Understand why agents go to conferences. For agents, going to conferences is as much about the opportunity to bond and network with other agents and authors as it is about finding new literary talent. Remember—it's not an agent's job to read your query letters. It's an agent's job to sell books. We read query letters and talk to unpublished authors in order to find great books to sell—it's a means to an end, not an end unto itself.

So when you see agents and editors hanging out together, understand that if we didn't have these opportunities, we might not be at the conference at the first place. The best conferences understand this phenomenon and schedule formal time for the faculty to interact with each other.

5. Don't do something that's going to put you in the LTS pile. Every agent has one. LTS stands for "Life's Too Short." So, although I really shouldn't have to say this, there are a couple of times that agents are absolutely, positively off-limits. Don't bug us when:

- We're on the way to deliver a talk. We're thinking about how to best deliver that talk, not about your specific project. After the talk, however, absolutely, positively buttonhole us.

- We're in a situation where we can't comfortably shake your hand. Examples: in the buffet line. In the pool. At the gym. In the restroom. (You'd be surprised. Every agent has horror stories, believe me.)

- Understand that no means no. If an agent tells you no, that's it. Move on. There are lots of good fish in the sea. No stalking allowed.

It's probably possible to write a whole book on what to do and not to do at a writers' conference. But I'll wrap it up here.

There are wonderful literary agents out there who can help you take your publishing success to a level that is difficult to obtain by yourself. The key is to know when you do or don't need an agent.

> Want to meet literary agents?
> Join us at the next Author 101 University.
> Use coupon code "MAM" to save half off
> Your tuition. details on the next event
> can be found at Author101.com

Mistake #15

Signing a Crappy Contract

We'll talk elsewhere in this book about not writing a crappy book. But now we're going to warn you to make sure you don't sign a crappy contract with any publisher. The landscape is littered with authors who were so excited to have a traditional publisher publish their book that they didn't take the time to read the fine print of their contract before signing it.

Then a couple years or so down the road they find that they can't do that audiobook version or make that movie deal or pursue any other opportunity that may come their way. Why? Because they signed over all the rights to their book when they signed that book contract.

If you determine a literary agent is right for you then this is an area that they are well versed in and can really help you out—they'll negotiate these things for you. But even if someone is negotiating on your behalf we feel it is important that you understand what the various rights are you may be dealing with. These can include:

- Copyright
- All Rights
- Subsidiary Rights
- Dramatic, Television and Motion Picture Rights
- Electronic Rights

Knowing the basic rights you have with your book and the terms used by the publishing world can help avoid some major disappointments in the future.

"Knowing your basic rights and the terms used by the publishing world can help avoid some major disappointments"

As the author of your book you own the copyright to that book, unless you have assigned those rights to a third party. Your copyright protection is automatic, without you needing to take any action. The moment your book is in finished form, whether in print or for electronic delivery, you are entitled to copyright protection.

As owner of a copyright what you really own is a "bundle" of rights consisting of multiple items. Each item may be pulled from the bundle and sold or assigned separately to any third party. If you give up all rights to your book then you are doing exactly that—giving it all away. The publisher can publish your book in any format without providing additional payment to you.

You retain the right to say you authored the book, but you lose all the other rights to the work, including the right to publish, market or distribute the work, to create derivative works, or to perform the work.

In a book publishing contract, subsidiary rights are all rights owned by you aside from the right to publish your book. Subsidiary rights are negotiable in a book contract and can cover such potentially valuable rights as movie, film, videotape and audiotape rights, book club rights, translation rights, electronic rights such as books on CD, courseware and foreign rights.

You may retain subsidiary rights so your literary agent can negotiate separate deals for each of the rights, or the subsidiary rights may be sold to the book publisher. Then it is up to the publisher to negotiate the rights. Every situation is unique and many literary agents or intellectual property rights attorneys advise you to retain the subsidiary rights on the grounds that they can obtain a more favorable deal for you than the publisher can.

The rights licensed when selling work for use in a play, television or on film are known as Dramatic, Television and Motion Picture Rights. A typical agreement awards the author 10% of the agreed upon selling price of your book in exchange for the exclusive right to market and produce the work. This is done as an "option" and the usual time limit for an option is just one year. If the option on your book expires and isn't exercised, you get to keep the money and are free to option your book to someone else. There is no guarantee that if you option your book that it will ever become a film, play or TV show.

The licensing of electronic rights to a book these days is, as you might expect, a hot topic. The optimal way to handle the electronic rights to your book is to clearly spell out exactly which electronic rights are being licensed and which are not. Electronic rights can encompass the rights to sell and distribute the work on CD, to sell ebook versions for the Kindle, Nook and other readers, to store your work in a database such as Lexis-Nexus, to publish your book work on the Internet and more.

To some extent the entire world of electronic rights is written on the fly by authors, editors and publishers. Eventually, the terms used will come to have standard meanings within the industry.

As an author you've got to have an understanding of the business basics of being an author. It's your book—shouldn't you have an idea of what your rights are? Whatever type of publisher you select to publish your book with, you need to read and understand all the terms and conditions involved with any contract that you sign. If you don't have a literary agent to represent you then at least get a lawyer to look at the contract.

There are a lot of parts to a traditional book contract with a publisher. There's an excellent article by Valerie Peterson we recommend you read covering the typical clauses contained in a book contract along with a brief description as to the purpose of each. You can find this article via a link from our resources page at MistakesAuthorsMake.com/resources.

Bottom line, it's your job as the author to make sure you know what you're getting yourself into before you get into it. It's a real "bear" to try to get the rights back to a book you've written that has gone out of print. Just ask Rick. And with the advent of the newer "print on demand" technologies some publishers will tell you that your book is never really out of print and they can refuse to release rights back to you even though they're doing nothing to promote your book in any way.

Watch out for the publishing pitfalls that can really bite you on the backside. Take the time to make sure you understand any contract you're considering signing so you don't give up something you didn't intend to give up.

Mistake #16

Failure to Register Your Copyright

You've poured your heart and your soul into writing your book and you're feeling great about what you've written. Then all of a sudden one day you're browsing through some website and you come across some words that sound so familiar. Then it hits you—they're *your* words from the book you recently wrote.

Naturally you're quite upset. You take a look around to see if any credit whatsoever has been given to you for your content. You find none. So what are you to do? And what should you have done, if anything, to protect yourself from being ripped off?

"Many people confuse copyrights, patents and trademarks"

The first thing you need to be sure is you understand the meaning of copyright. Many people confuse copyrights, patents and trademarks. There are some similarities between these three different types of intellectual property protection, but they are different and do serve different purposes.

Copyright (not to be confused with copywriting—the writing of sales copy) is a form of legal protection that is provided to the author of original works of authorship. This could include literary, musical, artistic, dramatic and other intellectual works that may have been published or not.

The Copyright Act of 1976 generally gives you, the owner of the copyright, the exclusive right to reproduce your copyrighted work, to prepare derivative works from your original, to distribute your work, to perform your copyrighted work in a public setting or to display your copyrighted work in public.

It is very important to recognize that this copyright protection protects the form of expression and not the subject matter of your writing. Copyrights are registered by the Copyright Office of the Library of Congress. The duration of a copyright depends upon when the original work was created. To view the details of the Copyright Act of 1976 visit the "Additional Reading" section on the MistakesAuthorsMake.com/ resources page online.

A trademark can be a symbol, a word, a name or a device that one uses in the trade with goods. It indicates the source of those goods and its intent is to distinguish them from the goods of others. Very similar to a trademark is what is known as a servicemark. A servicemark identifies and distinguishes the source of a service, rather than a product. The terms "trademark" and "mark" are often used interchangeably.

Trademark rights may be used to prevent others from using a confusingly similar mark. This does not, however, prevent others from producing the same goods or prevent others from selling the same goods or services under a clearly different mark. If you intend to use a trademark in interstate or foreign commerce you may register it with the Patent and Trademark Office.

There are some additional differences between a copyright and a trademark and we recommend a visit to the website LawMart.com for an excellent article on the differences between copyrights and trademarks and patents. Go to the "Additional Reading" section at MistakesAuthorsMake.com/resources.

LawMart.com also offers for just $3.95 a Copyright Cease and Desist Letter you can purchase and then modify, of course, to send to someone you feel is violating your copyright. Visit our Mistakes Authors Make Resources page online for a direct link to this letter.

> For a sample copyright cease and desist letter
> visit our resources section online at
> MistakesAuthorsMake.com/resources

As the owner of copyright you have the right to reproduce or authorize others to reproduce your work. This right is subject to certain limitations found in sections 107 through 118 of the copyright law. One of the more important limitations is the doctrine of "fair use." The doctrine of fair use has developed through a substantial number of court decisions over the years and has been codified in section 107 of the copyright law.

Section 107 contains a list of the various purposes for which the reproduction of a particular work may be considered fair, such as criticism, comment, news reporting, teaching, scholarship, and research. Section 107 also sets out four factors to be considered in determining whether or not a particular use is fair.

1. The purpose and character of the use, including whether such use is of commercial nature or is for nonprofit educational purposes.
2. The nature of the copyrighted work.

3. The amount and substantiality of the portion used in relation to the copyrighted work as a whole.

4. The effect of the use upon the potential market for, or value of, the copyrighted work.

The distinction between what is fair use and what is infringement in a particular case will not always be clear or easily defined. There is no specific number of words, lines, or notes that may safely be taken without permission. Acknowledging the source of the copyrighted material does not substitute for obtaining permission.

So what do you do if you feel you've been ripped off? A cease and desist letter seems like the logical place to start. But what if that draws no response from the offending party? Frankly, you'll have to decide how much time, energy, and more importantly, money you're willing to invest in an attempt to right the wrong. It can be a tough call.

Several years ago another company operating in the same market niche as a company of Bret and Bryan's clearly lifted some sales copy verbatim from one of our websites. It was a blatant copyright violation. But our analysis of the potential harm and the costs associated with trying to prove we were harmed substantially led to the decision to let the matter go. Was it the right call? Who knows? But it was the call we made because we decided we had more important things on which to focus our time and money.

You may face a similar decision at some point in your career as an author. It can be a tough decision. Only you can decide what the right course of action is for you in your situation. Certainly you should take the basic step of registering your copyrighted material. The last time we looked it was just $35 to register your copyright with the US Government.

And, if you've got more questions about copyright visit the copyright's office principal website at http://www.copyright.gov/help/faq/.

Expecting Other People to Do It For You

I n the information marketing world, of which books are a big part, there is a misguided belief that people will jump on your bandwagon and promote your product like crazy. Many authors think they can set up what is called an affiliate program and find people who will promote their book for a percentage of the sale.

The reality is that in almost all cases this simply is not going to happen. In theory, affiliate programs sound great. People who are your fans will come forth like crazy to help you sell your book because they love it that much.

"You will have to carry the bulk of the load in promotion of your book"

We all wish that were true, but the sad reality is that you yourself will have to carry the bulk of the load in promotion of your book. We'll speak later about the need for an on-going commitment to the marketing of your book. That commitment and the execution of that commitment fall squarely on your shoulders and no one else.

Let's consider affiliate programs for a minute. In the info marketing world most affiliate programs pay from 30% to 50% of the sales price of the book to the referring affiliate. That means on a $15 book you're going to give an affiliate anywhere from $4.50 to $7.50 of that book price as their commission. If you've got a great back end product or service that's extremely profitable and you're able to convert book buyers to clients than that may be fine.

But what you're battling for is the affiliate's attention. It takes as much effort to sell a $15 book as it does to sell a $500 product so where do you think an affiliate is most likely to focus his or her efforts? On a product they make $4.50 on or on one that they make $150.00 on? The choice for most people is fairly obvious.

Further, the running of an affiliate program adds an additional "hat" to the mix of the many hats you already have to wear. Now you're a sales manager and the management of a sales force (your affiliates) can quickly become a time consuming thing. Affiliates require continual attention in order to get them to promote and you have to invest the time and money to give them affiliate tools to promote your book with—things like banner ads, pre-written emails, Facebook posts and more.

Now if your book is a lead generation device for you and you can convert a significant percentage on the back end to higher ticket items then you may be able to get affiliates on board if they also get a cut of the sale on that higher ticket item also. But you'll need to be able to show them actual conversion percentages in order to even get most affiliate's attention.

Brendon Burchard did a great job of this with his book *The Millionaire Messenger* because he had his back end products in place and had a tremendous track record established that was attractive to affiliates. As we discussed previously, he knew the money was in the back end and was willing to reward affiliates handsomely for getting people into his funnel by helping with the promotion of his book.

It's certainly somewhere all authors would like to get but, unfortunately, if you're just starting out it's not going to be your reality. That's okay. Continue to build your platform and someday you can be there yourself.

Just know that initially you will be the one who has to drive your marketing engine. You'll have to learn how to drive traffic to your website and there are a number of ways to do that—pay per click advertising on sites like Google, Yahoo and Bing; Facebook advertising, and more. The landscape of online advertising is continually changing and it takes time to get up to speed on what works and what doesn't work on the Internet. You'll have some failures without a doubt. Don't let it get you down and keep on plugging ahead.

And don't forget about offline marketing channels. If you've done a good job of truly identifying who the target market for your list is then you can use those demographics to identify mailing lists (both physical and email lists) to potentially reach the audience you want to reach. Social media is an interesting beast. There are those authors that swear by the positive impact it has had in helping them build their platform and there are those that consider it a complete waste of time. Overall, we think it's a good tool in your marketing arsenal but it definitely shouldn't be the sole focus of your marketing efforts. We'll discuss the social media phenomenon later in the book.

You definitely want to be sure that your marketing efforts consist of more than one tool. We've seen entire businesses wiped out because they relied on one and only one marketing channel to drive traffic to their website. Then Google changed their algorithm and their website disappeared from the top of the search listings. Poof, business gone.

We could write an entire chapter about the inherent weakness of "one" for authors. Relying on only one marketing channel to drive online traffic. Bad. Relying on only one product to build your business. Bad. The supposed "Power of One" is a misnomer in the marketing world. It is a weakness, not a power.

While you are the primary driver of your book marketing efforts that doesn't mean that you are the one who has to do all the actual legwork. Consider the use of a virtual assistant or a marketing assistant to help you with some of the parts. The weakness of "one" in marketing also applies to you. If you're relying solely on your time to put all the marketing pieces in place than some critical things may not get done. It can become so easy to get distracted by life and forget about the importance of a continual, consistent marketing effort. Having others to help you with the day to day activities can be well worth it.

Just remember, it is your job to drive your marketing engine. Others won't do it for you and the sole reliance on affiliates to market your book for you is a recipe for failure.

Mistake #18

No Commitment to Continual Learning

We'll speak elsewhere in this book about the importance of attending live events for networking purposes and about the fantastic education you can pick up at events like Author 101 University and Author U. We can't emphasize enough how important it is for you as an author to have an ongoing commitment to increasing your knowledge. You must be a lifelong learner.

Knowledge of your topic, knowledge of marketing, knowledge of the publishing world, etc. The list could go on and on. If you have a true passion for sharing your message with the world and you know people would benefit from your message you owe it both to yourself and to your audience to continue to learn how to share your message most effectively. Aren't you doing those people who you can positively impact a disservice if you aren't?

Obviously live events are a great way to learn new things and recharge your batteries. But learning can occur via other avenues and you need to determine which avenue best fits you. We discussed elsewhere that in the information marketing world there are four primary "learning modalities." Each person typically has their primary preferred method of learning.

If attending live events is your preferred method for learning new information you are what is known as an "experiential" or "kinesthetic" learner.

If you'd rather curl up with a good book (and who wouldn't as an author) then your preferred learning style is reading.

If you'd rather listen to the audiobook version of material then you're an auditory learner and if you'd rather sit at home and watch the DVD of a training or view a webinar online then you're what is known as a visual learner.

There is no right or wrong method. What is wrong is not focusing your learning efforts on the modality that is the best fit for you. If you can't stand to listen to a CD why would you invest in an audio program to further your education? It's important for you to recognize in yourself the information consumption method that best feeds your need for continual learning. Then feed it!

If you prefer to feed yourself via live events there are two primary types of events—those that focus on the area of book marketing and publishing and those that focus more on the art of writing. A quick online search for "Writer's Conferences" uncovered a list of 98 such conferences in the United States alone that focus on some aspect of the art of writing. Each writing genre seems to have its own local and national writer's conference. Visit our resources page at MistakesAuthorsMake. com/resources for a link to writer's conferences.

On the book marketing and publishing side of things for live events you have:

Author 101 University – More info at Author101.com
Author U: More info at AuthorU.org

If you'd prefer to read a good book there are many fantastic resources you should have as part of your learning library, starting with Rick's series of Author 101 books.

- *Author 101 Bestselling Book Publicity: The Insider's Guide to Promoting Your Book--and Yourself*—Rick Frishman, Robyn Freedman Spizman and Mark Steisel
- *Author 101 Bestselling Book Proposals: The Insider's Guide to Selling Your Work*—Rick Frishman and Robyn Freedman Spizman
- *Author 101 Bestselling Nonfiction: The Insider's Guide to Making Reality Sell*—Rick Frishman, Robyn Freedman Spizman and Mark Steisel
- *Author 101: Bestselling Secrets from Top Agents*—Rick Frishman and Robyn Freedman Spizman
- *Author 101: The Insider's Guide to Publishing From Proposal to Bestseller*—Rick Frishman and Robyn Freedman Spizman
- *Guerrilla Marketing for Writers: 100 No-Cost, Low-Cost Weapons for Selling Your Work*—Jay Conrad Levinson, Rick Frishman, Michael Larsen and David Hancock
- *Write: Why? Marketing for Writers*—Kenneth Atchity, Ridgely Goldsborough and Rick Frishman
- *Show Me About Book Publishing: Survive and Thrive in Today's Literary Jungle*—Judith Briles, Rick Frishman and John Kremer
- *The Entrepreneurial Author: Achieving Success and Balance as a Writer in the 21st Century*—David Hancock, Jay Conrad Levinson and Rick Frishman

- *1001 Ways to Market Your Books*—John Kremer
- *APE: Author, Publisher, Entrepreneur-How to Publish a Book*—Guy Kawasaki and Shawn Welch
- *How to Sell Books by the Truckload on Amazon.com—Book One and Two: Get More Sales—Get More Reviews!*—Penny Sansevieri
- *52 Ways to Sell More Books!*— Penny C. Sansevieri
- *Author YOU-Creating and Building the Author and Book Platforms*—Judith Briles
- *Snappy Sassy Salty: Wise Words for Authors and Writers*—Judith Briles
- *Dan Poynter's Self-Publishing Manual: How to Write, Print and Sell Your Own Book*—Dan Poynter
- *Dan Poynter's Self-Publishing Manual: How to Write, Print and Sell Your Own Book (Volume 2)*—Dan Poynter
- *Writing Nonfiction: Turning Thoughts into Books*—Dan Poynter
- *Writing Your Book*—Dan Poynter
- *Publish and Profit* – Mike Koenigs

For you auditory learners:

- *Author 101: A Complete Get Published Curriculum—From Top Industry Insiders Audiobook*—Rick Frishman and Robyn Freedman Spizman
- *Creating and Developing Your Author and Book Platform Audio CD*—Judith Briles

For you visual learners:

- *Author101Online.com*—Our online membership community with on-going live training webinars from industry experts like Tom Antion, Alex Carroll, Jim Howard, Starley Murray, Hobie Hobart, Justin Spizman, Wendy Lipton-Dibner, John Kremer, Jeanette Cates, Paul Colligan, Carol McManus and others.

Our good friends Daniel Hall and Connie Ragen Green also do regular training on Kindle Publishing and other publishing related topics. Check out DanielHallPresents.com and ConnieRagenGreen.com for more information. And the legendary John Kremer offers a wealth of resources via his site at Bookmarket.com. We'll be adding additional resources as we become aware of them to our resources page at MistakesAuthorsMake.com/resources.

It's often said that the definition of insanity is to do the same thing over and over again and expect different results. If your book marketing efforts aren't getting you the results you want then what are you going to do differently to change your results?

The pros are out there—learn from them! There's no need for you to reinvent the wheel when you can walk in the footsteps of those who have walked that path before you. Study Rick Frishman, John Kremer, Dan Poynter and the other masters whose wisdom can help you cut your learning curve tremendously. You don't have to walk that trail alone.

"Your on-going commitment to learning will pay massive dividends over the long haul"

Your on-going commitment to continually increasing your knowledge about book marketing and publishing will pay massive dividends over the long haul. Simply by reading this book you are demonstrating some of that commitment—just be sure you always keep your momentum moving forward.

3 video trainings on book marketing are yours
absolutely free at Author101Online.com

Mistake #19

No Continuity Revenue

One of the biggest challenges an author/information marketer faces is how to best monetize the knowledge that they wish to impart to the world. Your book should primarily be a front end product—a lead generator—that brings people into your circle of influence, where you'll sell them additional products and services.

One of the absolutely best things you can offer to your readers who want more of you is some type of subscription service, be it a newsletter, CD of the month or a membership site where people have access to additional content online from you.

Going into a month already having a good idea of how much baseline income you have in place via your paid subscribers can take a tremendous burden off of you as an author. You're not in perpetual "what can I sell now" mode like you see from some of the online marketers who seemingly go from new product launch to new product launch, always looking for that next infusion of cash.

----

*"Newsletters are one of the single most overlooked
methods of developing continuity revenue"*

Newsletters are one of the single most overlooked methods of developing continuity revenue. You can certainly do a digital only version of a newsletter, but an actual printed newsletter that is mailed to your subscribers can really set you apart from your crowd of potential competitors. That offline touch is so often overlooked by marketers because it does involve a bit more work. Not only are you delivering your great content via your newsletter, it also gives you the ability to sell your other products and services via ride along offers and ads within your newsletter.

You can even outsource the development and delivery of your newsletter to others. There are companies that specialize in providing newsletters where all you have to do is provide a few minor tweaks to make it your own. This is a lot easier than starting with a blank piece of paper each time. But a physical newsletter is still a great and frequently overlooked source of continuity revenue.

A CD of the month is another way to share your content with your followers. If your crowd prefers auditory learning then give them what they prefer via CD. For just a few dollars a month you can put your name in front of your readers (listeners) again and again and again. Bret and Bryan offer a service called Disc Delivered (DiscDelivered.com) that you can check out if you're in need of shipment of physical CDs or DVDs,

You can even combine either a newsletter or CD with a membership site as a "stick strategy". Bret and Bryan are members of a coaching program called AM2 based primarily around Internet marketing. Depending upon the level of membership, each person receives an actual full-color physical magazine and a CD of the month. These offline touches greatly extend the average amount of time a member remains a member.

> For more information on the AM2 Internet
> coaching program visit AM2.com

With membership sites you'll need to determine how much content to include within your site and how much information each person will have when they join your group. Do you give access to all content to everyone immediately when they join or do you "drip" content out on some predetermined schedule. Both can be effective. It's simply a matter of determining which is the best fit for you.

Like books and other information products, you've got to remember that the key to a membership site is "consumption." How well you get your members to be involved and to return to your site to consume your information is crucial if you want them to remain a member on-going. You've got to drive them back to your site regularly via emails announcing what's new and what's upcoming. Emails aren't just a sales tool—they're a great product consumption tool also.

If you do a newsletter you can also use your newsletter to drive people back to the membership site. We believe that regular, on-going communication with your members is important. We know there are some marketers that operate under the premise that they don't want to "talk" with their members because that'll just remind them they're paying a monthly membership fee and therefore might cancel their membership. Frankly, we think that's BS. Your membership site, like your book, should be about delivering outstanding content to your readers and trying to "hide" hoping they don't cancel their membership is the wrong way to go about things.

You must not allow your membership site to grow stale. You should regularly add new content on some fairly regular schedule, whether it's weekly or monthly. Nothing turns members off more quickly than returning to a site and finding that nothing has changed at all. Stay ahead of the game as much as possible and don't hesitate to use your connections with others in your niche to help provide additional content when needed.

As an author you undoubtedly have a tremendous amount of content you can deliver. How can you "slice and dice" your book's content to provide additional material for your membership site. You can include content in audio, video, pdfs and other formats within your membership site to address the different learning modalities we discussed previously. Repurposing of content that you already have in different formats is a great way to come up with additional content for a membership site.

If you're doing a membership site we recommend you do it with Wishlist Member software. Our good friends Stu McLaren and Tracy Childers developed Wishlist and it is an easy to use platform that sits right on top of Wordpress, which is the website platform we recommend. It's extremely powerful and extremely cost effective. Check it out at WishlistMember.com.

Whether it's a membership site, a newsletter, a CD (or DVD) of the month or something else such as a service that people pay monthly for (e.g. web hosting, shopping cart, etc.) the importance of developing some form of continuity revenue for authors is important. Many of the well-known on-line marketers today continually bemoan the fact that they didn't develop some type of continuity revenue earlier in their business. They left lots of money on the table because they were always continually chasing that next sale.

Section 3

WRITING YOUR BOOK

Mistake #20

Writing a Crappy Book

We mentioned earlier in the book Rick's pet phrase about your book—*"It doesn't have to be perfect, it just has to be."* Truer words were never spoken.

Does that mean you want to put out a poorly written piece of crap? Of course not. Your book should be good, maybe even great. But it doesn't have to be perfect. Naturally, you want to be sure you don't have glaring grammatical errors and misspellings so take the time to get your manuscript proofread and cleaned up appropriately.

The pursuit for perfectionism has stopped more good books and other information products in their tracks then almost anything else. Let me tell you a story.

A few years ago I was involved with the development of an information product on how to put on seminars—get butts in the seats, deal with the hotels, etc. There were five people involved in the development of this product and one particular team member insisted on dotting every "i" and crossing every "t" eighteen times.

A great product that should have been completed and sent to market in January drug on into February, then March, then April, and then on into May and June. All because of the desire to have the "perfect" product. This pursuit for perfectionism totally killed the momentum of the group. Interest in the product waned and what was really a great product in terms of content never achieved the level of success it could have.

"Perfectionism can kill your profits"

Perfectionism can really kill your profits. Because a book not out in the marketplace isn't making you any money. It's not generating you any new readers, any new leads, or helping you to build your following in any way.

What are some of the other things that make for a "crappy" book aside from the obvious typos and grammatical errors that seem to creep into books? Some might say it's bad writing. But it's impossible to define bad writing because no one can seem to agree on a singular definition. We all know it when we see it, but we all see it subjectively.

What makes you put a book down? There was an interesting survey in a July, 2013 blog post from GoodReads where they queried their members on this specific question. Here were the reasons their readers gave as to why they put a book down.

- 46.4% of members—Slow, boring
- 18.8% of members—Weak writing
- 8.8% of members—Extremely stupid
- 8.5% of members—Ridiculous (or nonexistent) plot
- 4.9% of members—I don't like the main character

- 3.8% of members—Inappropriate, makes me uncomfortable
- 3.2% of members—When an author is committed to doing something I hate
- 2.7% of members—Bad editing
- 2.5% of members—Any combination of the reasons above
- 0.5% of members—Immoral

Now it seems to us this list applies mainly to a fiction book, but there's a lesson here for any author—fiction or non-fiction. If your book comes across as any of the above on this list you run the risk of your book being considered bad. Not somewhere you want to go.

Further lessons can be learned from GoodReads survey of its membership with the question "What keeps you turning pages?" Here's that list:

- 36.6% of members—As a rule, I like to finish things
- 25.2% of members—I have to know what happens
- 13.4% of members—It's a compulsive habit
- 9.3% of members—Come back to it at the right time
- 7.4% of members—It's the same as films: I have to watch them to the end, no matter how inane they might be
- 3.2% of members—I judge a book by its ending
- 2.6% of members—I'm committed to the series
- 2.3% of members—I'm usually pleasantly surprised that an author can pull it out in the end

Again, very interesting. Obviously some people will stick through with you to the bitter end of a book but why do you even want your book to be a battle for them to consume? Make it a good book—make it one where they want to keep turning the pages.

For another perspective on this I asked legendary book marketer John Kremer, author of "*1001 Ways to Market Your Book*" what, in his opinion, made for a "crappy" book. Here were his top three:

#1 The book doesn't have stories. People are always drawn in by stories and the lack of stories in a book makes it uninteresting.

#2 Lack of depth of content. Coverage of the topic is so superficial that people just don't really get drawn in to your message.

#3 Lack of a good cover. If you can't even get them to pick your book up off the shelf to look inside it doesn't matter how great the writing may be—you probably have a crappy book.

John made it a point to emphasize that a great cover can help to overcome less than stellar writing in regards to making a book attractive to a prospective reader. But, on the flip side, in almost all cases a greatly written book cannot overcome the hurdle of a poor cover. We'll talk in more depth about book covers later in the book.

If there is one piece of advice we would give to writers it is "Keep writing". As a first time author it is depressing to pour your heart and soul into a bit of writing only to learn upon re-reading what you've just written is as dreadful as it comes. The secret is to keep at it until it's not so dreadful anymore. And then to keep at it some more until it's good.

Remember, it doesn't have to be perfect but you do want it to be good. You want to strive for perfection but there must come a time where you recognize that good enough is good enough and it's time to get your book out to the marketplace.

Poor Book Title

In copywriting it's well-known that the headline is the most important element of any sales copy. The job of your headline is to catch the interest of the reader and compel him or her to read on.

In *Scientific Advertising* the late great Claude Hopkins wrote "The purpose of headlines is to pick out the people you can interest. You wish to talk to someone in a crowd, so the first thing you say is 'Hey there, Bill Jones' to get the right person's attention."

David Ogilvy, author of *Ogilvy on Advertising*, said 'Headlines get five times the readership of the body copy. If your headline doesn't sell, you have wasted your money.'

"Your book title IS the headline for your book"

Let's face it, the title you choose for your book is really the headline for your book. The job of your book title is to catch the eye of a prospective reader and cause him or her to want to read further—on to your back cover copy and then hopefully they'll open your book on up and start perusing the inside.

But what makes a good book title? Or a great book title? Rick says that optimally your book's title should be 3-5 words at the most. It makes it more memorable in most cases and also allows you to have a domain for your book that isn't excessively long. Remember, you can have a subtitle that elaborates further on the major premise of your book, but the main title itself should be fairly short.

Beauty is in the eye of the beholder they say and it's kind of the same way with book titles. But there are some suggested guidelines to help you hone in on the best title for your book. Creating a good title for your book helps you ensure it will stick in the minds of your prospective readers. A good book title should be considered a marketing tool for your book.

If working with a traditional publisher many different people will have an opinion as to the consumer appeal and the potential effectiveness of your book's title. This could include publicists, editors and sales reps. Sometimes even book buyers for the major booksellers will weigh in.

However, if you are self-publishing your book then the decision on your book title is yours and yours alone, so you need to understand what your book title needs to achieve. Ideally your book title will create some type of emotional response from your potential readers. And while book titles cannot generally be copyrighted you'll want the title of your book to be unique.

For a non-fiction book title, the writing of a good title usually means crafting a concrete promise—a clear benefit statement as to what your readers can expect to learn from your book. Here are a few straightforward examples:

- *Getting Things Done*
- *Get Noticed… Get Referrals*
- *Relationships Raise Money*
- *No B.S. Direct Marketing*
- *Endless Referrals*

Non-fiction books typically also get a subtitle. Sometimes it's hard to get the whole idea of a book into the few words of a book title, which is why someone invented subtitles. The subtitle expands on the promise of the title and plays a clarifying role in many cases.

Here are the books above that included a subtitle on their cover:

- *Getting Things Done: The Art of Stress-Free Productivity*
- *Relationships Raise Money: A Guide to Corporate Sponsorship*
- *No B.S. Direct Marketing: The Ultimate No Holds Barred Kick Butt Take No Prisoners Direct Marketing for Non-Direct Marketing Businesses*

You can see how the addition of a subtitle in these instances further elaborates on the main title and makes the entire book sounds more inviting. *Stress-Free?* Cool. *A Guide to Corporate Sponsorship.* Got it. *No Holds Barred Kick Butt Take No Prisoners.* I like that.

But what if you're writing a novel or other fiction title? The writing of a successful, eye-catching title for fiction or narrative non-fiction book such as a memoir also involves reflecting the book's promise. What you're crafting is the promise of an entertaining read.

A good novel or memoir title should reflect the contents of the book in a manner that evokes an emotional reaction or curiosity from your reader. Your prospective book buyer should feel like they want to know more.

So how do you know when you're on the right track with your book title? If you have a list of followers survey your list. Give them several options to choose from and see which draws the most response from your list.

Go back to our old friend Amazon and study the titles of the best-selling books in your niche. Are there specific keywords they're using in their titles that you should consider for your book? You won't want to title your book exactly the same as another book or you'll create possible confusion but you can use those other titles for inspiration.

Remember, even if you come up with a great book title you can't copyright it, so others can use the same title on their book.

On our resources page at MistakesAuthorsMake.com/resources you'll find a link to what readers of GoodReads felt were the best book titles. Surprisingly, several of the top titles were longer, which emphasizes our earlier beauty is in the eyes of the beholder comment.

E. Haldeman-Julius did a fascinating study years ago on how the title of a book impacted its sales figures. Haldeman-Julius sold a series of Little Blue Books back in the 1920's for a nickel apiece and he sold them via direct mail by title alone. He sold over 100 million Little Blue Books and published his sales results based on title in a fascinating book titled *The First Hundred Million*, which is available on Bret and Bryan's online bookstore at SFSBookstore.com.

Creating a great book title is hard. Resist the urge to rush the process. Sure, sometimes the perfect title will just jump out at you from the beginning. But usually it takes a bit longer and the time spent to find the best title can play massive dividends.

Mistake #22

Bad Cover Design

Somewhere in the neighborhood of 3 million new books will be published this year. Let's face it, it's tough to stand out in this size of a crowd. You're not only competing with all the new titles coming out, you're competing with all the books that came into the marketplace in previous years.

So why would you want to handicap yourself in any way in your marketing efforts? A bad cover design is definitely a handicap to the marketability of your book. But how does one determine what is bad? What some may see as a poor cover, others will think is wonderful. It's all so subjective.

According to our good friends Kathi Dunn and Hobie Hobart of Dunn + Associates Design, specialists in strategic book cover design, studies show that customers glance at a front book cover for 8 seconds and a back cover for 15 seconds before deciding whether to buy it. That means you have a whopping 23 seconds to really grab their eye and draw them in. Not a ton of time.

"Customers glance at a front book cover for only 8 seconds"

And that's in a traditional brick and mortar bookstore. Online, it may be as little as 3 to 8 seconds.

Further, Kathi and Hobie point out that there are lots of details that can make or break a book cover, things such as:

- Emotion of color
- Power of typography
- Importance of the spine
- Technical requirements of a bar code
- Intricacies of book printer specifications
- Fine points of today's ebook covers

Book cover design is certainly one of those areas where the proverbial "you get what you pay for" comes into play. Trying to do your book cover design yourself is, for most people, a fool's errand. Unless you're an outstanding graphic designer and you fully understand all the subtleties associated with the bullet points above from Kathi and Hobie you're far better off handing this task off to the professional.

If you just don't have the budget to hire a professional cover designer then be sure you have a solid understanding of the elements of good cover design.

We've all seen book covers we just don't like. Maybe it's because they suffer from poor aesthetics, or they're poorly rendered. Or maybe the cover is just too busy or plain dull. Some covers misrepresent the text they introduce, unintentionally or intentionally promising a book they can't deliver. A book cover has many jobs to do, with responsibilities to the book itself, the publisher, and the reader.

Your book cover isn't only a picture, it's your packaging. It should immediately communicate to your reader the kind of book it contains so it needs to fit in with the packaging that similar books use. Be sure you spend plenty of time on Amazon searching for other books in your genre. Look to see what common elements the covers have. You'd be surprised at how similar they actually are.

The front cover of your book is certainly the most important piece of your cover design. But the spine and back cover designs aren't far behind. In a traditional bookstore the majority of books are displayed spine out rather than front cover out so you've got to make that spine stand out also. If you're doing a hardcover book with a dust jacket the front and back inside flaps are also important.

Once you've determined what kind of image you want on your cover it is definitely worth getting a high quality image you can use. By high quality we mean a picture with a minimum resolution of 300 dpi (dots per inch) so that you cover looks great printed. You can't simply grab a low 72 dpi resolution image from a website and use it on your book cover. It'll look pixelated and you won't be happy with the end result.

There's a big difference in the quality of amateur and professional photos and graphics so it is best to resist the urge to choose a lower quality image for sentimental reasons. There are some great stock photo websites such as StockFresh.com and iStockPhoto.com where you can find images with a creative commons license that are very inexpensive.

If you're going to do your own images you'll need to have experience with programs like Photoshop or Adobe InDesign. These aren't cheap programs and can be a bit challenging to learn. So if you aren't already a graphics designer and these tools aren't already part of your toolbox think twice about heading down this path. If you are not an experienced designer you're better off aiming for simple and elegant rather than going for something complicated. Covers can quickly become cluttered if you go overboard.

So what elements must you absolutely include on a book cover and what elements are nice to have but not necessarily need to have? The most important element of your cover is your book title. Shorter titles are better, anywhere from 3 to 5 words in length. Then you need a subtitle that dives deeper into the benefit(s) your reader will get from your book.

Here are some examples from Rick's and Bret's previous books:

- *Where's Your Wow?: 16 Ways to Make Your Competitors Wish They Were You!*
- *Author 101 Bestselling Book Publicity: The Insider's Guide to Promoting Your Book… and Yourself*
- *Author 101 Bestselling Book Proposals: The Insider's Guide to Selling Your Work*
- *View From the Back: 101 Tips for Event Promoters Who Want to Dramatically Increase Back-of-the-Room Sales*
- *Networking Magic: How to Find Connections that Transform Your Life*
- *50 Biggest Website Mistakes: Secrets to Getting More Traffic, Converting More Customers & Making More Sales*

So your front cover will carry your book title, subtitle, and your selected graphic primarily. But it also might include if your design supports it pithy testimonial from a person who is well known in your industry and/or a seal or other designation of any award your book may have won, such as "New York Times Bestseller" or something similar.

We know how important the front cover of your book is. But in some ways your book's spine may be even more important. The spine is the first thing people will see almost always but it is the spine that draws the potential reader in in the first place.

Consider your book's spine and cover in tandem when you're packaging your book. You want the two of them to be cohesive in design and image. The design of your book's spine should be interesting and should give the prospective reader a hint as to the genre of your book. You want your spine to stand out amongst the other titles in your genre.

You want a spine that is striking. Color is important, especially for thinner books. You don't have a lot of product "real estate," so you need to make your spine space count. The best way to do this is by using a brighter color that will stand out from the books that may be sitting beside it on the shelf.

Think about your potential readers and how you want them to feel when glancing at your book on the shelf. Different colors means different things and this may have an impact on how your potential buyer views your book.

The contrast between the colors on your spine may be even more important than the color itself. The books that really seem to catch the eye use contrasting colors, such as a light colored font on a darker background or vice versa. You want the spine of your book to really "pop" even at a distance.

For the spine of your book use a sans serif font. These "blocky" texts seem to stand out more than thinner, serif fonts. It is generally advisable to avoid script fonts or other fonts that are difficult to read. If your book is thin than a bold, simple text is even more important. You don't have any room such as bigger books have to put graphics on your spine, so be very careful of your text selection.

Think about how you can make your spine interesting. The design should be striking but not too overwhelming. You're going to include your title, your name, and possibly the logo of your publisher if space permits. If you have a wider spine then definitely consider some graphics on the spine to help yours jump off the shelf.

Now let's move on to the back cover. Obviously, the color scheme of your front, spine and back all need to combine together into one cohesive unit. But what information should you have on the back? One must be your ISBN barcode. This is what retailers scan so someone can purchase your book. You can buy blocks of ISBNs online at Bowker. com. You convert your ISBN into a barcode graphic and that graphic is placed usually in the lower right corner of your back cover.

Generally the back cover of a book will contain a brief synopsis of the benefits the reader will gain from reading your book. Usually just a paragraph or two with some quick and easy to read bullet points highlighting the major things.

Then your back might also include any or all of the following depending on how your design comes together:

- Brief bio of the author
- 2 or 3 "rave reviews" for your book
- Author photograph
- Website URL with some incentive to visit you online

Again, it depends on how your design comes together as to how much information you want to include on your back cover. You have to watch the overwhelm factor on the back cover as much as you do on the front.

It is a bit difficult to put into words what a great book cover looks like. It's one of those "you know it when you see it" type things. But resist the urge to rush through the cover design phase and just throw something together at the last minute. Your cover design can have a dramatic impact on how well your book will sell. Check out the resources at the back of this book or online at MistakesAuthorsMake. com/resources for our recommendations for book cover designers.

Mistake #23

Writing a Book that is Not Easily Consumable

You can still write what most would consider a good book yet have it fall short of being a great book simply because it wasn't as consumable as it could be. Information products, including books, are all about "consumption" and if your book isn't optimized for maximum "readability" then you won't have the same level of success you could otherwise.

I love to go into a bookstore and browse the shelves, especially the books in the marketing and business sections. I'll scan the covers and spines that are visible and, if a title sounds interesting enough, pick the book up and thumb through to the first chapter.

If I look at that first chapter and see that it is twenty or more pages in length in all likelihood I'll put the book back on the shelf and won't buy it. Why? Because it looks like it's just too much work to read. You want people to feel a sense of progress as they read your book and if your chapters are so long that they discourage reading on you're making a big mistake.

---

*"Make sure your book doesn't suffer
from 'consumption obstruction'"*

A book like this suffers from what I call "consumption obstruction." If you're like a lot of people you might do a little reading before you go to bed. If you pick up a book and scan through the next chapter to see how long it is and you see that it's too long then you put the book down and don't even start reading that next chapter.

You're far better off having three chapters that are about seven pages each rather than one chapter of twenty pages. People are far more likely to read a chapter, see that it is only another seven pages to complete the next chapter, so they keep reading. And so on.

Remember, if you can't even get them to consume your book the chances of them coming back to you to buy your next book or some other product or service that you have to offer drops dramatically. It really is all about consumption.

So what are some of the other things you need to consider to make your book more readable, and therefore, more consumable?

One thing you certainly need to consider is the demographics of the audience you want to reach. Let's say you're writing a book aimed at, for example, the baby boomer market. Then you're marketing to a crowd that is largely dealing with bifocals and trifocals and gradually deteriorating eyesight. So if you or your book interior designer select a font size of anything less than 11 point you're creating readability issues for some of your potential audience.

According to Wikipedia, here are the "Keep Out of Trouble Rules" regarding font usage in a book.

- Use 11-point Palatino for text.
- Use 14-point Helvetica for chapter titles and 12-point Helvetica for section headings
- Use unusual fonts only for short items, e.g., the title and author's name on the cover, or for chapter titles.
- Don't use too many fonts. Three should be enough for almost any book.
- Check books you like the look of, and see which fonts they use. Half an hour in a bookstore looking at fonts can be very useful and enlightening.

During the layout of your book you'll need to determine how you want to break your paragraphs apart for better readability. Let's demonstrate.

"Here's a paragraph where sentence after sentence has been packed together and the paragraph seems to run on forever. Run on paragraphs such as this can make it extremely difficult for your readers to consume the information you want to share with them. And when you're trying to build your platform as an author if you do anything that makes it more of a challenge to consume your information the more challenges you are putting in front of yourself to achieve success. Don't make it any harder than it needs to be—there are plenty of other things you're going to have to deal with that are challenging enough. Run on paragraphs are easily dealt with simply by breaking you paragraphs into two or more paragraphs. Our opinion is a paragraph should be no longer than three or four sentences before you start a new paragraph."

Now compare that to this:

"Here's that same basic paragraph broken into two separate paragraphs. The sentences don't run on and the paragraph doesn't seem to run on forever. Don't make it difficult for your readers to consume the information you want to share with them.

When you're trying to build your platform as an author if you do anything that makes it more of a challenge to consume your information the more challenges you are putting in front of yourself to achieve success.

Don't make it any harder than it needs to be—there are plenty of other things you're going to have to deal with that are challenging enough. Run on paragraphs are easily dealt with simply by breaking you paragraphs into two or more paragraphs.

Our opinion is a paragraph should be no longer than three or four sentences before you start a new paragraph."

Which seems more readable? The split paragraph obviously. So it's simply a matter of laying out your book slightly differently in order to make it more consumable for your reader.

If you didn't catch it in that big block paragraph above we recommend that the maximum length of a paragraph be three or four sentences before breaking for a new paragraph. You'll need to decide with your layout person if you're going to have a blank line break between paragraphs or not. The pro is it generally increases readability. The con is it increases your overall page count so your book printing costs may be slightly higher.

Another thing you can do to increase readability of your book is to include call-outs or bulleted lists to the eye a break from the same thing page after page after page.

"This is an Example of a Call-Out"

Call-outs can be a quote or a salient point about that chapter you most want people to remember.

The "Keep Out of Trouble Rules" above is an example of a bulleted list. Both call-outs and bulleted lists should be used in moderation, but both are great tools to improve the readability of your book.

Avoiding "Consumption Obstruction" is something to which very few authors give thought. Yet, turning your book from a good book into a great book may be nothing more than improving your layout to make your book more readable.

Mistake #24

Poor Interior Layout

Ever pick up a book, flip it open and find it basically unreadable? It's like it actually hurts your eyeballs to read that book. You can't put your finger on exactly what's off, but you know something is off.

We talked earlier about the importance of cover design for your book. Almost as important, and many would argue equally important, is the interior layout of your book. If your layout isn't "reader friendly" than the chances of them actually reading your book and coming back to you for other books, products or services of yours goes way, way down. Like to slim or none.

There are so many things within interior design that can negatively impact the readability of your book. You can do 9 out of 10 things perfectly, but the one thing you overlook can quickly undo those 9 things you did right.

So what are some of those interior design factors that can bite you in the butt if you're not careful? We discussed a few of these earlier but, in no particular order, here are some additional things you need to watch out for:

Too Small of Font

Think of the target audience for your book. Is it teens, 20 somethings, Gen-Xers, Boomers? As we age most of us find our eyesight gets worse. We've gone to bifocals or trifocals and it can become a real challenge to read things. So if the boomer market (50+) is your intended audience why would you use font that's so tiny it's hard to read? You want to make it easier to consume your book, not harder. Typically, older readers and younger reader prefer larger font.

If your ideal reader isn't in the older or younger set than 11 pt. or 11.5-sized font seems to be the norm these days.

Too Many Different Fonts

We've all seen it. The book where an interior design person seemed to be on a campaign to see how many different font types that could put within a single book. It's like the book from Hell—an endless journey through FontLand. Mixing and matching fonts like crazy is nuts—it makes your book extremely difficult to read. Choose a primary font for the body of your book and stick with it throughout. It's okay to have a different, fancier font for your headlines or subheadlines, but make sure it's still readable.

A popular font these days for the interior of books is Palantino. Other widely used fonts include:

- Book Antiqua
- Georgia
- Goudy Old Style

- Adobe Garamond Pro
- Bookman
- Century Schoolbook

Overwhelming, Blocky Text

We cover this in elsewhere in the book so we won't repeat it all here. Bottom line; avoid big chunky blocks of text that intimidate the reader.

Ragged Right Text

Almost any professional looking book utilizes justified text, where the right edge of the text is all aligned. It gives your book a much more professional look. Let's take a look at Abraham Lincoln's famous Gettysburg address in ragged right format and justified format to see the difference.

"Almost any professional looking book utilizes justified text"

Ragged Right:

Four score and seven years ago our fathers brought forth on this continent a new nation, conceived in liberty, and dedicated to the proposition that all men are created equal.

Now we are engaged in a great civil war, testing whether that nation, or any nation so conceived and so dedicated, can long endure. We are met on a great battlefield of that war. We have come to dedicate a portion of that field, as a final resting place for those who here gave their lives that that nation might live. It is altogether fitting and proper that we should do this.

But, in a larger sense, we cannot dedicate, we cannot consecrate, we cannot hallow this ground. The brave men, living and dead, who struggled here, have consecrated it, far above our poor power to add or detract. The world will little note, nor long remember what we say here, but it can never forget what they did here. It is for us the living, rather, to be dedicated here to the unfinished work which they who fought here have thus far so nobly advanced. It is rather for us to be here dedicated to the great task remaining before us—that from these honored dead we take increased devotion to that cause for which they gave the last full measure of devotion—that we here highly resolve that these dead shall not have died in vain—that this nation, under God, shall have a new birth of freedom—and that government of the people, by the people, for the people, shall not perish from the earth.

Justified:

Four score and seven years ago our fathers brought forth on this continent a new nation, conceived in liberty, and dedicated to the proposition that all men are created equal.

Now we are engaged in a great civil war, testing whether that nation, or any nation so conceived and so dedicated, can long endure. We are met on a great battlefield of that war. We have come to dedicate a portion of that field, as a final resting place for those who here gave their lives that that nation might live. It is altogether fitting and proper that we should do this.

But, in a larger sense, we cannot dedicate, we cannot consecrate, we cannot hallow this ground. The brave men, living and dead, who struggled here, have consecrated it, far above our poor power to add or detract. The world will little note, nor long remember what we say here, but it can never forget what they did here. It is for us the living, rather, to be dedicated here to the unfinished work which they who fought here have thus far so nobly advanced. It is rather for us to be here dedicated to the great task remaining before us—that from these honored dead we take increased devotion to that cause for which they gave the last full measure of devotion—that we here highly resolve that these dead shall not have died in vain—that this nation, under God, shall have a new birth of freedom—and that government of the people, by the people, for the people, shall not perish from the earth.

You can see how justified text is a bit cleaner and easier on the eye.

Widows and Orphans

In book layout, widows and orphans are words or short lines at the beginning or end of a paragraph, which are left dangling at the top or bottom of a column, separated from the rest of the paragraph. There is some disagreement about the definitions of widow and orphan; what one source calls a widow another calls an orphan. *The Chicago Manual of Style* uses these definitions:

Widow
- A paragraph-ending line that falls at the beginning of the following page/column, thus separated from the rest of the text.

Orphan
- A paragraph-opening line that appears by itself at the bottom of a page/column.
- A word, part of a word, or very short line that appears by itself at the end of a paragraph. Orphans result in too much white space between paragraphs or at the bottom of a page.

Whether you call it a widow or an orphan you want to avoid it in your book layout. It makes your book look amateurish.

Chapter Starts Alternating Between
Left and Right Facing Pages

There may be some disagreement on this one, but in our opinion, a new chapter should always start on a right side page in a book. Concurrently, all odd-numbered pages in a book should always be on the right. Does it improve the readability of your book in any way? Probably not. But we think it looks better.

No Subheads

You need to remember that a lot of people read by skimming over the text in a book. If the major topic in a particular chapter has key secondary points that, when combined together, make up your major point you should highlight the start of your major secondary points through the use of subheads.

Poor Leading

In book layout, leading (pronounced ledding, not leading) refers to the distance between the bottom edge of successive lines of type. The term originated in the days of hand-typesetting, when thin strips of lead were inserted into the forms to increase the vertical distance between lines of type.

In consumer-oriented word processing software, this concept is usually referred to as "line spacing" or "interline spacing."

Text set "solid" (no leading) appears cramped, with the highest point of some letters almost touching the bottom point of letters from the previous line. This lack of white space between lines makes it difficult for the eye to track from one line to the next and hinders readability.

In book layout single spacing or less between lines is discouraged, as it makes it too difficult to read. Double spacing is considered too wide, so 1.15 or 1.5 spacing is generally suggested.

No Hyphenation of Text, Causing Gaps and Spaces on the Page

When you're doing justified text (right and left margins both straight) you can have some longer words that kick down to the next line due to their length. This can cause wider gaps than desired in the previous line as it spaces the words out to fit across your page. You can avoid this by making sure you have hyphenation turned on during the layout process.

Margins Too Small, Making Your Book Hard to Hold

I recently borrowed a book from the library, a paperback of one of the Jack Reacher novels by Lee Child. The layout person had apparently not taken into account at all how readable the book would be, as the left margin of every right side page and the right margin of every left side page in the book was jammed up so tight to the spine of the book you almost couldn't open the book wide enough to see all the text.

At a minimum you should have a ½" margin around all sides of your text. Some books go as wide as 1", so you'll have to decide what is right for you.

Poor Kerning

In book layout, kerning is the process of adjusting the spacing between characters in a proportional font, usually to achieve a more visually pleasing result. Kerning adjusts the space between individual letters. In a well-kerned font, the two-dimensional blank spaces between each pair of characters all have a visually similar area.

No Name Capture Mechanisms Built Into Your Book

W e discussed back in an earlier chapter the importance of making sure you're not writing your book for the wrong reason—to make money directly from the sales of the book. We discussed the benefit of your book serving as an entry point into your entire product mix and how the real money from a book was made on the products and services people purchased from you that were a follow up to your book.

That means your book is what many would consider a lead generation product. It's designed to introduce people to you, to get them into your "funnel" which you hope will lead to the sale of those other products and services. Some would say your book should be used as a business card and you shouldn't hesitate to get your book into the hands of as many people as possible.

But there is a problem you need to overcome with your book if you want to turn it into a high performing lead generation device for you.

That problem is that if someone buys your book online, say at Amazon, or they buy your book in a retail bookstore like Barnes and Noble or Books a Million, you have no idea who purchased your book.

They do not pick up the phone and call you or shoot you an email to tell you the name and contact information of the book buyer. It simply doesn't work that way.

That's why you, as the author, need to build into your book what are called "name capture mechanisms." What are name capture mechanisms? In most cases they are invitations from you to the reader to come to a website for additional bonus content.

---

*"You must build into your book ways to capture
the info of the Amazon or bookstore buyer"*

When your reader comes to that website they'll usually have to opt in by providing you their name and email address in exchange for that bonus content. Your bonus content could be many different things including:

- Audio content such as an interview of you
- Special PDF reports that expand upon some topic in your book
- Video content
- Checklists or other tools related to your topic
- Newsletter

You're really only limited by your own creativity as to what might make suitable bonus content for your readers. Ideally, your bonus content should be directly related to the core content of your book. Someone reading your book about, for example, improving your relationship with your spouse probably wouldn't have much interest in a bonus special video about Michael Jordan's greatest career dunks on the basketball court.

We're frequently asked how many times within a book should you try to drive the reader to your website in an effort to capture their name and email address. It, to a large extent, depends on the length of your chapters. If you have shorter chapters then every 3-4 chapters is probably sufficient. If you have long chapters you may even be able to do one per chapter. Any more than that and we think it can start to become a bit annoying. But it's your book, so include as many name capture mechanisms (also called bounce back offers) within it as you want.

Some always include their offers for additional content at the end of a chapter but there is nothing wrong with using callouts or what are called "Johnson Boxes" in the middle of a chapter to draw attention. Here's an example of a Johnson Box.

> For a free subscription to Rick's weekly newsletter
> and to receive his "Million Dollar Rolodex"
> visit RickFrishman.com

It's so important to make sure that anywhere online you are driving people to from your book is fully functional. You don't know how many books we've seen offering bonus content that failed miserably on this front. You type in the URL they're directing you to and the page isn't even there.

Your book should be among your best list building tools. Please make sure any resource you're directing people to within your book is fully ready to go. Otherwise it just becomes a missed opportunity.

How much information should you attempt to capture from an online visitor who came from your book? No more than you intend to use in your on-going marketing. The less information you request the more people are likely to complete the request and opt in to your list.

You absolutely must have their email address. In most cases, their first and last names are also requested. Some will request only the first name. It's your call.

If the bonus content is something you'll actually be physically mailing them then you have to capture address information also. Digital bonuses are usually the way to go. Just bear in mind the more information you ask for the lower your response rate will be.

Once you've decided on your bonus content for your printed book you're pretty well locked into those items because once they're in print they're in print forever. But, if you have an ebook version of your book, say for Kindle, you can swap out your bonuses from time to time and test the market to see which bonuses are more attractive to your readers and therefore, bringing more people from your book onto your list.

This obviously requires you to track things carefully online to see what the winners and losers are but the effort can be well worth it as you strive to grow your list of followers.

We can't stress enough how your book should be among your better list building tools. And the only way it can help you to increase your platform and the size of your list of followers is by using your book to drive them online where you can capture their name and email address. Give careful thought as you are writing your book as to what other information would your readers be interested in that would inspire them to visit your website and give you their name and email address.

Your ability to convert the casual reader into a real fan by getting them to provide you their information is critical for building your platform and impacting even more people with your message. "Name capture mechanisms" or "Bounce back offers" are your keys to greater impact.

3 video trainings on book marketing are yours
absolutely free at Author101Online.com

No Branding

Did you realize that, as an author, you are a brand? Further, any book or book series you may write may also become a brand. Consider these well-known business book authors:

- Seth Godin
- Larry Winget
- Jeffrey Gitomer
- Rick Frishman
- Dan Kennedy

If you hop over to any of their websites (just type in TheirName. com, e.g. RickFrishman.com) you'll see clearly that they are the brand. They've authored a number of books usually centered around a particular theme and, while their books are certainly an important part of their site, they themselves are front and center as the brand. It's important that you own your own name as a domain if at all possible so people can easily find you. If you have a common name like Bill Smith and you can't get BillSmith.com then try TheBillSmith.com or BillSmithAuthor. com as backups.

In some cases for our authors listed above, a series of books they've authored has also become a brand. Witness Jeffrey Gitomer's *Little Books of Selling* series, Dan Kennedy's *No B.S. Series* or Rick's *Author 101* series for examples. In the fiction world look no further than J.K. Rowling's *Harry Potter* series or Stephenie Meyer's *Twilight* series to witness megabrands. In the latter cases the book series has become a far bigger brand than the authors themselves.

Most authors give very little thought to what their brand should be. They just let things kinds of evolve on their own without any forethought or planning. And most don't have any real concept of what a brand is. They think if they get some nice logo done by a graphic artist that is their brand. Not true. A brand is way more than simply a pretty logo.

"A brand is more than a logo"

In fact, if you look at most of the authors listed above websites you won't even find what most people would call a traditional logo. You'll find primarily a large picture of that author as the focal point of their main page. One of the things you'll need to decide early in the game is what you want to focus your branding efforts on. Yourself? Your book? Your series of books? Your company? Something else?

A lot of it will be determined by what your bigger picture is. If you're a public speaker or a consultant or a coach and your book is primarily a sales tool to help promote your higher ticket services then the focus should be primarily on you. If you don't have the back end products or services then the focus may be more on your book. More likely, some combination of the above.

So, if a brand is more than a logo then what is it? According to Sergio Zyman, author of *The End of Advertising As We Know It*, a brand is essentially a container for a customer's complete experience with the product or company. So, a logo could be part of it but all of the following can also be part of your brand:

- Your tag line
- Your product packaging
- Your customer service response times
- Your email communications
- Your pricing
- Your guarantee
- Your book cover
- Your history
- Your reputation

According to Seth Godin, one of our business book authors referenced previously, "A brand is the set of expectations, memories, stories and relationships that, taken together, account for a consumer's decision to choose one product or service over another." Further, Seth says "If the consumer (whether it's a business, a buyer, a voter or a donor) doesn't pay a premium, make a selection or spread the word, then no brand value exists for that consumer.

Your brand is what your customer (in your case—reader) perceives it to be and every point of interaction between your reader and you frames that perception of what your brand is. And once you've "created" your brand you need to be true to your brand. If you deviate from your brand in some way you do so at great peril to your long term health.

Here's a story to illustrate this. A few years ago Bret sat down for lunch at an event with a guy who was in the financial services market. Over the course of a few years he had developed a fairly sizable email list—around 55,000 people. He had communicated with his followers on a regular schedule with his messages having a consistent tone and feel.

Then one time he decided he wanted to "jazz up" his marketing and he hired an Internet 'guru' to help him craft a message to his market. But the guru didn't bother to look at the tone of previous communications with this list and the message they came out with was a very hard sell, which was totally opposite of how this list had been trained they would be communicated with. It began happening almost immediately—unsubscribe—unsubscribe—unsubscribe. When all was said and done a list that had been about 55,000 in size shrunk to a list of right around 5,000 people. Ouch!

What happened? This marketer had created a brand image for his email followers and the frequency and tone of communications with that list was a significant part of that brand. So when they came in with a hard hitting message that was the polar opposite of what they had been trained this guy's brand was all about it was a major disconnect and he killed that list.

So, a few words to the wise. Make sure that anyone you bring onto your team to assist you with your marketing in any way is well aware of the brand you've created and doesn't do anything, even unintentionally, to damage your brand's reputation. Doesn't matter if it's a consultant, a marketing assistant, a virtual assistant or anyone else. They need to understand your brand.

If your brand is to be you personally then you'll also need to give thought to what is your long term strategy. If you want to build a company that you might eventually sell and the entire brand is a personality brand based on you it becomes very difficult to sell. If, however, your branding is based on a "company" then you have a more sellable asset. If you want to build a company you can hand down to your children someday and the brand is all you and something happens to you what happens to your company? In most cases, the company simply dies when an owner dies.

Branding is very important for any author. Make sure you figure out early on what and how you want to brand yourself and your book or books. It can pay big dividends in the long term.

Mistake # 27

Doing an Ebook Only

According to *Forbes* Magazine 19.5% of all books sold in the United States are Kindle titles. That's a lot of ebooks! Further, ebooks now make up about 30% of all book sales, of which Amazon has a 65% share within that category.

USA Today reports that the number of ebooks sold last year grew by *only* 43%. Why do they say "*only*"? Because in previous years ebook growth was measured in triple digits. American Publishers and the Book Industry Study Group show that 457 million ebooks were sold last year. That's up 4456% since 2008, when just 10 million ebooks were sold.

Other sources have reported that ebook sales have surpassed physical book sales, so sometimes it's hard to know who to believe. But, in either scenario, there's no arguing that there has been massive growth in the sales of ebooks over the last few years.

So, obviously, one needs to be putting their books out in ebook format. The rush to the digital world is immense, with Kindles, Nooks, iPads and other ebook reading devices selling in the millions of units per year. Many people consume books only in electronic format these days and the lack of an ebook version of your title would be a mistake.

But a far bigger mistake in our opinion is offering your book only in digital format. Let's take a closer look at those numbers above. If what *Forbes* says is accurate, with 30% of the books sold being ebooks that means that 70% of the books sold are still old fashioned hardcover or softcover printed books. In fact, according to *USA Today*, last year there were 557 million hardcover books sold, which surpasses by itself the sales quantity of eBooks. By the time you add in paperback sales the difference is even more significant in the volume of physical vs. ebook sales.

"70% of books sold are still hardcover or softcover printed books"

Michael Pietsch, CEO of the Hachette Book Group, says, "In all the talk about ebooks, we often lose track of the fact that more than three out of four books sold in the U.S. are still printed ones." He also cites a survey from last year that found that half of all readers had no interest in buying ebooks and that the vast majority of people who buy ebooks continue to buy print books as well.

With the significant growth of ebooks over the last several years we find a lot of authors who want to dive into what we call the digital-only pond. In the information-marketing world we've seen many influential marketers make the move to a digital only platform, sometimes with disastrous results. Here are a couple of case studies to illustrate the impact having a physical version of an information product had on the sales and the stick rate of that product.

A well-known marketer was selling a home-study course that consisted of a manual and a set of CDs for $497. She decided to convert that product to digital delivery only at that same $497 price. Yet, she had the foresight to continue to offer a physical version of her product, albeit it at a higher price—$697. An amazing 80% of her customers were willing to spend the additional $200 to receive a physical version of the product. They still wanted something tangible they could hold in their hands.

Another example—a pair of marketers were selling a high priced program ($3000) on how to create information products. This was for a digital only version of the product. For an additional $500—or $3500 total—you could also receive a physical version of this product. In this case 40% of their customers were willing to spend an extra $500 to get a physical version. Not as impressive as the 80% in our first example but still very impressive nonetheless.

But what was even more eye-opening to us was the impact that it had on the stick rate of the product. People that purchased the digital only version of this product requested a refund at the rate of 22%. Those that opted for the physical version in addition refunded at a rate of just 8%. So even after their hard costs of producing and getting this product into the hands of their customers they put a lot more money in their pocket and kept their product into the hands of more customers by having a physical version.

Should you offer a digital version of your book? Undoubtedly. Should you offer only a digital version of your book? No, no, no, no, and no. There's an illusion that the move to digital only would be much more profitable for publishers of books and information products. After all, if you don't have the hard costs of printing and the delivery costs to put the product into the hands of your customers you'll make more money, won't you?

A few years ago a number of newsletter publishers got caught up in this dive into the digital only pond. They converted their physical newsletters to digital only delivery because they believed they would make more money. The result? Unsubscribe, unsubscribe,

unsubscribe. People still wanted a physical newsletter. They'd been "trained" that the deliverable was a physical item and then all of a sudden it wasn't. Most of those publishers have returned to the physical format for their newsletters.

We do think it's a good idea that if someone buys your book from you that they receive both a physical and digital version of your book for one price. That way they get the immediate deliverable in addition to the physical goods. Remember, people don't want to buy a book. They want to buy a solution to the problem they have. So, if your book is, for example, about curing some health issue they might have they want that information now. So the digital/physical combination offers them the best of both worlds.

Ebooks will continue to have a massive impact on the book-publishing world. Just remember that so much of your potential audience would still prefer to curl up on the couch with a good old-fashioned physical book and turn the pages, one at a time.

Forgetting to Put Disclosures/ Disclaimers in Your Book

L et's face it—we're a litigious society. People are seemingly suing each other over the most trivial of things and anything that doesn't go right is always someone else's fault. As an author you've got to protect yourself, as best as possible, from this sad reality.

We're all familiar with all persons fictitious disclaimer in which a work of media states that all persons portrayed in it are fictitious. This is done to reduce the possibility of legal action for libel from any person who believes that he or she has been libeled via their portrayal in the work (whether portrayed under their real name or a different name).

Such a disclaimer often reads similarly to the following:

All characters appearing in this work are fictitious. Any resemblance to real persons, living or dead, is purely coincidental.

The wording of this disclaimer differs from jurisdiction to jurisdiction, and from country to country, as does its legal effectiveness.

What we're talking about, more importantly, is the scenario where your book promises some type of result—whether it is a financial return, a health benefit, improvement in a relationship or anything else. You are potentially opening yourself up to be sued by someone who read your book and didn't receive those results.

We can't repeat, for example, an earnings disclaimer here verbatim for copyright reasons. But go to any website that sells a product or service related to making money or promoting weight loss or some other health benefit and scroll down to the footer of the main page on their website. You should find a link to their earnings disclaimer to get an idea of what other people are doing. You should not copy someone else's disclaimer word for word but you should be able to modify what they have to suit your needs. Work with your legal professional to do this.

There are a couple different products on the market that can help you with this. Our good friend Armand Morin has a product called Auto Web Law that has cut and paste disclaimers and other documents you can use on a website or in a book. Be sure to insert your specific information in the appropriate spots, of course. For more on this go to AutoWebLaw.com. Last we checked the price was $147 for this software.

There's a similar product titled Website Law Forms (WebsiteLawForms.com) that is a bit pricier. You decide which may be the best solution for you.

Another common disclaimer you'll see in books reads as follows:

"The Publisher and the Author make no representations or warranties with respect to the accuracy or completeness of the contents of this work and specifically disclaim all warranties, including without limitation warranties of fitness for a particular purpose. No warranty may be created or extended by sales or promotional materials. The advice and strategies contained herein may not be suitable for every situation. This work is sold with the understanding that the Publisher is not engaged in rendering legal, accounting, or other professional services.

If professional assistance is required the services of a competent professional person should be sought. Neither the Publisher nor the Author shall be liable for damages arising herefrom. The fact that an organization or website is referred to in this work as a citation and/ or a potential source of further information does not mean that the Author or the Publisher endorses the information the organization or website may provide or recommendations it may make. Further, readers should be aware that internet websites listed in this work may have changed or disappeared between when this work was written and when it is read."

This disclaimer example was provided courtesy of David Hancock of Morgan James Publishing (MorganJamesPublishing.com).

If your book is in one of those grey areas—making money, health benefits, etc. and you think you're immune to potential lawsuits or the scrutiny of the FTC and other government organizations, think again. One has to look no further than Kevin Trudeau, the author of *"Natural Cures 'They' Don't Want You to Know About"* and infomercial fame. He's currently serving a term in federal prison for promoting various unsubstantiated health, diet and financial remedies.

"Your disclaimer is your first line of defense against the average guy or gal on the street who might read your book

----

Remember that just having a disclaimer in your book or on your website doesn't mean you won't get sued, especially if you piss off the Federal Government. But it's definitely one of your first lines of defense against the average guy or gal on the street that might read your book. Will people read your disclaimer? Probably never. But you still need to have it in your book and on your website.

If you're writing a non-fiction book your absolute first line of defense is to be entirely truthful in your book. Don't make claims that aren't true and that you don't have the documentation to fully backup if push comes to shove. And even that won't necessarily protect you if the FTC or some other governmental agency puts a bulls eye on your back and decides they're coming after you.

Now, don't keep from writing your book for fear of being sued or becoming the target of some governmental investigation. You've got a wonderful story to share and the world needs to hear your story. Just don't overlook important things such as disclaimers that should be a part of your book regardless of the subject matter of your book.

Seems as if everyone is suing everyone these days. Bloggers are being sued for writing bad reviews that are ranking high in Google™. Authors are being sued for not delivering manuscripts for books on which they were given an advance. Authors are being sued for self-publishing after previously publishing a book with a big name publisher. It's crazy out there.

Of course, there are no guarantees you'll never be sued as an author. But if you mind your p's and q's and dot your i's and cross your t's then you're doing the right things and should be fine.

Section 4

MARKETING YOUR BOOK
BEFORE IT'S WRITTEN

Failure to Develop a Book Proposal/ Book Business Plan

So, are you going to treat your book as a hobby or as a business? Are you going to play at it or are you serious about building your platform and using your book as a key pillar in the structure of that platform? It's put up or shut up time as an author—are you ready?

If you're committed to your book and the role it will play in helping you to spread your important message to the world then the next step is to take the time to develop a book proposal for your book.

If you are seeking a traditional publisher a book proposal is absolutely required. But, even if you intend to self-publish, going through this exercise will help you to build a better business around your book and, in all likelihood, enable you to write a better book.

Here are the elements of your book proposal and what should go into each section:

#1 Cover Letter — This is the introduction to your book proposal. If you're sending the proposal to an agent, you should have already made contact and gotten them to agree to review your book proposal. Like any cover letter, your book proposal cover letter should be short and punchy and give your reader the best highlights of:

- Why the market needs your book.
- Who is the target audience for your book?
- Your author bio highlighting your media platform and other connections to the book's subject. How many people do you already have a relationship with in some way.
- What you anticipate your finished book will look like: how many pages, what format, will it contain illustrations or photographs
- When you'll deliver a finished manuscript
- Your writing style and tone
- What the rest of the proposal contains

#2 Overview of Your Proposed Book - The overview should give a robust overview of the book, focusing on marketplace need, and how the market need will be filled by the book you're proposing. What's important here is that the agent or editor sees that you know the market and have a clear vision for your book.

#3 Author Biography—What your background is in more depth. Why you are uniquely qualified to bring this specific book to the market.

#4 Target Market for Your Book—Here is where you'll show you know the market and who your potential readers are. If you can, quantify how many potential readers there will be for your book.

#5 Competition for Your Book—Here's where you'll show more of your insights by knowing what other books are in the marketplace that could be considered competition for your book. Then, show how your completed book will be better than any of the rest of them. Highlight how the other books in your space all lack some key element that your audience needs—a key element that your book will include.

 # 6 Table of Contents/Chapter Summaries—This is essentially a fleshed-out Table of Contents, showing the flow of your ideas throughout your book. You'll give overviews of each chapter via short bullet points or very short paragraphs. This might change after you sell the book to a publisher, but you should still show you have a complete, initial vision for your book.

#7 Sample Chapter—This representative chapter will give a prospective literary agent and/or acquiring editor an idea of your narrative writing and your ability to communicate your ideas in a coherent, cohesive manner.

Your book proposal may also be a key component of a more in depth book business plan. Why would you develop a business plan for your book? Because you need to recognize your book is a business. Now we're not going to go into depth on business plans in this book—there are a lot of great resources on business plans available. But a book business plan can actually serve three primary functions for you.

#1—Your Action Plan

A book business plan can help to move you to action. You may have been thinking for years about writing your book, but the process may seem too daunting. A book business plan will help you to pull apart the pieces of starting the business around your book and examine each piece individually. So, instead of one large overwhelming problem, you have a sequence of smaller problems. And by solving the small problems, the large problem is automatically solved. So writing a book business plan can help to move you to action by breaking down a seemingly insurmountable task (writing and marketing your book) into many smaller, less intimidating tasks.

"Writing a book business plan can help move you to action"

#2—Your Road Map

Once you have started the business around your book, your book business plan can be an invaluable tool to help keep you on track and moving in the direction you want to go. In the hustle and bustle of daily life, it is very easy to lose sight of your objectives and goals—your book business plan can help to keep you focused. A book business plan can also serve to help publishers and others to understand your vision.

#3—A Sales Tool

Your book business plan can serve as a sales tool. A well-written book business plan can serve to sell people close to you on the benefits of proceeding with your book. Perhaps the most important reason to write a book business plan is that it requires you to engage in a rigorous, thoughtful and painful process that is essential before you start a viable venture.

It requires you to answer hard questions about your book—why is there a need for your book? Who is you target market? How is your book different from what's already out in the market? What is your competitive advantage? How profitable can your book be and what are the cash flows? How should you fund development and marketing of your book?

We believe development of a book proposal and a corresponding book business plan are important elements if you want to have a larger impact with your book. Be sure you invest the necessary time to do it right.

A great resource to help you with
writing a book proposal that is
absolutely free can be found online
at RicksBookProposalWiz.com

No List Building Efforts in Advance of Publication

L egendary information marketer Dan Kennedy calls them your "herd." Book publishers call it your "platform." Others call them your "fans" or your "followers." It doesn't matter what you chose to call them—it's all about the number of people that you already have a relationship with in some way before your book is published.

The depth of the relationship is also an important factor. 1,000 paying members of an online membership site in your area of expertise (and about the topic your book will be about) is much more impressive than 1,000 followers on Twitter. These "members" obviously have a much deeper relationship with you then a group of Twitter followers.

Why is it so important to have this list? Simply put, it is that group of people who have already raised their hand in some way and identified themselves as someone who is interested in you. Who, therefore, is then likely to be someone who will buy your book.

We've heard at various book marketing and publishing conferences such as our own Rick Frishman's "Author 101 University" that traditional publishers typically like authors to have a platform of at least 100,000 followers before they'll give them serious consideration for publication.

"Traditional publishers want you to have
a platform of at least 100,000 followers"

That 100,000 can be across multiple channels—Facebook fans, Twitter followers, LinkedIn contacts, YouTube channel subscribers, Blog Talk radio show listeners, email list subscribers, customer database, etc. But 100,000 is still a fairly significantly sized list. So how do you start to build a list of 100,000 followers?

In terms of relative strength, a list of previous customers who have already purchased something from you related to the topic of your book is at the top of the heap. If you can show a publisher you already have a sizable customer list who, in all likelihood, will buy your book, then you jump to the front of the line.

Unfortunately, most of us are not in this enviable position where we already have a large list. So we need to begin to build our list of followers so that we become a more attractive partner for a traditional publisher. We talk about the different publishing models elsewhere in the book because this is less of a factor if you're looking at self-publishing or what are called "vanity" presses.

If you don't have any list building efforts in place you need begin immediately. View every interaction you have with a person or a group as an opportunity to build your list. For most the primary push will be via online methods, as most of the channels we mentioned earlier involve the Internet in some way. But don't neglect offline methods. If you attend a live event use it as an opportunity to meet new people and to collect their business cards in order to add them to your list.

Make sure the information of the people you've met at an event is entered into a database so you'll have the ability to easily reach out to those people at a later date. Capturing their name along with an email address are probably the most critical bits of information you need to gather. But if you can also capture their mailing address, phone number and other information by all means, do so. This will give you the ability to reach out in other ways then via email if you want to when you're ready.

If you're speaking at a Rotary meeting figure out, in advance, what you can do to capture the names of the people in the audience. Can you offer some type of ethical bribe such as a special report or an audio program they can download to the audience in exchange for their contact information? Obviously you need to be sure the event host is on board without whatever you're considering doing, but most are happy to accommodate you since you're sharing your expertise with their group.

The same is true for any trade show at which you're exhibiting. What are you going to do to attract people to your booth and what can you offer them in exchange for their contact information? Sometimes, it can be easy to get lost in a big crowd at a trade show, so you need to be creative with what you're going to do to attract them to your booth.

In the online world this "booth" is a website that people will visit. On this website it is common to have what is called an "optin box." This is where your online visitors will opt in to be on your email mailing list. And, just like in the world of physical trade shows where you need to "bribe" people to visit your booth and exchange their information for something they consider of value, you need to do the same online.

So what can you offer your potential followers of value that they would like to receive in exchange for providing you their name and email address? Many call this your "bribe." Maybe it's a special PDF report about the topic of which your book will be about. Maybe it's an audio download where you talk about your area of expertise. Maybe it's a free + shipping offer where they actually pay a few dollars to you in exchange for a physical disc you mail them that contains your content. See Bret and Bryan's site DiscDelivered.com if you're considering something like this.

Maybe it's even a free chapter of your book. Whatever you choose, as a rule, the more information you require them to give you in exchange for your "bribe" the lower your response rates will be. So if you don't intend to market to them later on via direct mail then don't attempt to capture their physical mailing address. You don't need it and requiring it will hinder your list building efforts.

Your optin box should appear what we call "above the fold" on the main page of your website. That means it is visible on their monitor as soon as they come to your site—they don't have to scroll down to find your optin box. But this optin box should also be placed at other spots on sub-pages within your site. You want to provide yourself more than a single opportunity to get them to optin.

Another important consideration is to make sure when you're writing your book that you make it a list building mechanism for all your future books. When someone buys your book on Amazon or at a traditional retail bookstore you don't have any idea who bought your book. The seller doesn't provide you with the buyer information.

So you need make sure to include what are called bounce back offers in your book to which people can respond. Just like the online bribes we talked about already, a bounce back offer is an attempt to drive them to your website where they'll optin to receive whatever it is you offered in your book. You need to make every attempt you can to get your current book buyers onto your list in order to be able to market future books or other products and services you may have to offer to them.

Your list building efforts needs to be a continuous, on-going thing. It's not something you do for a month or two and then stop. You need to always be building your list. Always.

Need a system to manage the list you'll be building?
Check out RedOakCart.com.

No On-going Communications with the List You're Building

As you continue to build your platform and list of followers it is critical that you recognize the importance of communicating with your list on a regular basis. Your lists will grow cold and the responsiveness of your lists will decline rapidly if you don't nurture them by communicating with them on a regular basis.

You'll notice that we said lists. Plural. You should have multiple lists based on how they came to be in your world. Met them at a specific event? That's a list. Met them at a different event? That's a different list. They opted in online for a email newsletter of yours? That's a third list.

Of course you'll want to have a "master list" on which everyone may reside. But you'll want to segregate your lists based on how they came into what is called your "marketing funnel" because you may want to communicate with those lists in different ways. Let's say you spoke at a Rotary meeting and talked about topic "A". Those people that gave you their contact information at that event are most interested in topic "A" and therefore, your on-going communications with this list should be largely based around topic "A."

But let's say you later spoke at a trade conference in your industry and the primary focus of your presentation was topic "B." Those people who came to be on your list via their attendance at this trade show should have as their primary focus of your on-going communications topic "B." The "hot buttons" of each group may be different so you may want to communicate with each group a bit differently.

How you communicate with your various lists is typically done by what are called "autoresponders." Autoresponders are pre-written messages that are delivered by email to those people on your list. These can be queued up to go out to your list members at pre-established time lapses from the date they initially joined your list.

It is entirely up to you as to whether all people who are added to your lists will receive the exact same messages or not based on how they came to be on your lists. It is certainly less work to take everyone through the same autoresponder message sequence but there may be some situations where different messages would be called for. It's your call.

As we mentioned, autoresponder messages are delivered by email. Pretty much any email system should have the capability of allowing you to pre-schedule a series of out-going messages to your lists. Popular systems these days that include both your email system and your ecommerce functionality (your online shopping cart that allows you take orders) include Infusionsoft, 1 Shopping Cart, Premium Web Cart and Red Oak Cart.

Others opt to separate their ecommerce and their email functionality into different systems. Popular email only platforms include AWeber, Get Response, Mail Chimp and Sender.info. Each approach has its pros and cons and you'll need to decide which approach best suits your needs first. Then, which specific provider within whatever approach you selected is the best solution for you.

Whatever solution you select you'll need to determine how frequently you want to communicate with your various lists. It is important to be consistent, as consistency helps you to build the 'know, like and trust' factor you want your list to have with you. The more they know, like and trust you the more apt they are to be to buy your book when it's ready to go. Or to take advantage of other products and services you may have to offer.

----
*"Consistency in communicating with your list is
what builds you that 'know, like and trust' factor"*

Your list members will come to expect a certain tone of communication from you and it is important to be pretty consistent with that tone. You'll need to decide what mix of content vs. sales offers you want to have in your email communications with your list. We certainly believe the mix of content vs. sales should be fairly heavily weighted on the content side and we're talking anywhere from a 5:1 up to a 10:1 ratio of content vs. sales.

Why is it so important to be consistent with your tone? Remember our story about the financial services marketer who saw his list plummet from a size of 55,000 + down to almost 5,000? A large part of the reason this happened, in my opinion, was the tone of communication from this marketer changed from what his audience had been trained to expect from him over the years.

That's why it is critical that if you're going to have anyone work for you in some capacity that will be communicating with your list that they be aware of how you've communicated with your list in the past. It doesn't matter whether it's a guru, a secretary, a marketing assistant, a virtual assistant or anybody else. They need to know your history of communication with your list.

We've referred to the consistency of tone your messages should have. The consistency of delivery is also an important factor. Some aggressive marketers we know mail their lists an offer nearly every day. Others we know seem to be very hit and miss as to when they communicate with their lists, if they are even communicating with their lists at all.

While we feel daily messages may be a little much, if that's the route you want to go just be sure you are consistent with that. We believe you should be communicating with your lists at least once per week on average. And it is so important to make sure you pre-write your messages and get them scheduled into your autoresponder system in advance so you don't have the mental burden every few days of having to come up with a new message.

We have some autoresponder series that are pre-written out to two years in advance. Knowing that it is all automated and ready to go allows us to focus our energies elsewhere.

Remember, it doesn't do you any good to build a list if you're not going to nurture that list by communicating with them on a regular basis. When your book is ready to come out you want your list members to be excited about its release and to be the first ones in line to buy it.

Communication is the key.

> Training webinar on email marketing
> from Bret and Bryan at:
> InfoMarketingTraining.com/EmailMarketing.
> use the coupon code "MAM1" to receive this
> $47 training webinar absolutely free!

No On-going Commitment to Marketing

S o many authors we know pour their heart and their soul into writing their masterpiece and then they simply... stop. They think that their work is done and they rush their manuscript off to their literary agent or publisher and relax.

If that is you then, first of all, congratulations on finishing your book. You've completed the first big step. You should pause briefly to celebrate completion of this important milestone. It's a big deal. But recognize that it is only one step. Your book will need to be marketed—it will not sell itself.

Marketing requires a commitment of both time and money. Chances are, a lot of the time investment will be of your own time although there may be some marketing activities you can outsource to others. But the major thing you need to recognize is that it requires an on-going commitment that should, in reality, begin many months before your book is published.

It's so easy each day to get bogged down in the little details of your business that you forget to invest any time in actually building your business. Michael Gerber of "*The E Myth*" fame describes it as working in your business rather than on your business.

The solution, according to our colleague and Internet marketing legend Armand Morin, is what he calls "Five-Minute Marketing." He makes sure he spends at least five minutes every day on some business-building marketing activity. Maybe it's an email promotion to his list. Or maybe it's a couple phone calls to potential joint venture partners to get a commitment to participate in your upcoming new book launch. Or maybe it's lining up an article writer to generate 50 new articles related to the topic of your book.

"Make sure you spend at least five minutes every day on some sort of business building activity"

It doesn't matter what it is as long as you're consistently applying some effort every day to activities that will help you to grow the business of your book. If you have employees, then the development of a myriad of processes and procedures will be critical to your long term success.

These processes and procedures are certainly business building activities. But these may or may not be marketing activities, so amongst the full complement of business building activities make sure you include something within the marketing realm. Your future success depends upon it.

Here's a quick list of marketing opportunities you might do:

- Post something to your blog
- Do an affiliate training call
- Send an email promotion to your list
- Write a new article and submit it to the article directories

- Do a guest post on someone else's blog
- Call your top joint venture partners and get a commitment to help you promote your upcoming book
- Send thank you cards to your biggest customers
- Be a guest speaker on a teleseminar or webinar
- Speak at a live event
- Schedule advertising in a suitable ezine
- Submit a press release
- Contact a media contact about your book
- Write a sales flyer on your book to go out with all other products you're currently shipping

This list is certainly not meant to be all-inclusive, but it should help you to stimulate your thinking.

And "Five-Minute Marketing" doesn't mean you have to do it all yourself. If you're building a company, then have one of your team members handle the marketing responsibilities. Just be sure someone in your organization is investing some time in marketing every day.

As we discussed, your marketing efforts will require an on-going time commitment. They will also require a money commitment. One of the key questions literary agents and publishers ask potential authors pretty early in the process is what kind of budget they have committed to assist in the marketing of their book.

Rick is a big believer in you should have at least $5,000 committed in advance to help you in your marketing efforts. That demonstrates to potential publishers your solid belief in your book and that you are going to put a serious effort into helping them to sell your book. Bottom line is they don't really help you sell your book that much—the marketing falls to you.

If funding of your marketing efforts is an issue you may want to give consideration to this relatively new concept called crowd funding to help you with your book. There is a new platform called Pubslush designed specifically for authors that seems to be catching on. Check it out at Pubslush.com.

However you fund your book marketing efforts the key thing is a consistency of effort. You should develop a marketing planning calendar to help you keep on track with your marketing efforts. You need to keep track of what you've done and the results of those efforts as best you can. If you just intend to sell a few copies to your family and friends then don't worry about it. But if you want to have maximum impact with your message you need to be marketing to a larger group.

We speak elsewhere in this book about using speaking to build your platform. Even if you are not speaking at any events currently you need to make an on-going commitment to attend live events to network. Your best joint venture partners, super affiliates, clients, etc. will come from the group of people who you've taken the time to get to know by being where they are.

You can build a book publishing empire on your own. But it's a lot easier if you have relationships with the movers and shakers in the industry and the place you get to know these people are at live events. If you're not attending two to three live events each year we believe you're truly stunting the growth of your information marketing business. At a minimum get to Rick's own "Author 101 University twice a year to recharge your batteries and meet new people that can help you in your efforts.

Many people classify themselves as what they do. They say "I'm a plumber." Or, "I'm a lawyer." What they need to recognize is that what they really are is a marketer of plumbing services or a marketer of legal services. Same for you—you're not just an author—you're a marketer of your book.

Not Using Social Media Properly

Nothing seems to stir up as much controversy in the book-marketing world as the ongoing debate over the value (or lack of value) of social media. Some authors claim massive success in using social media to build their platform while others eschew it as a total waste of time.

As with all things, the truth for most of us probably lies somewhere in the middle. There is no doubt that social media is very popular. You've got Facebook, you've got Twittter, you've got LinkedIn and Pinterest and Google Plus and Instagram and more. Some new social media platform that all new and experienced authors "must" be on seemingly pops up every other week.

How's one to keep up with it all?

Read an interesting piece recently by legendary marketer Dan Kennedy in the August 2014 issue of the *GKIC No BS Marketing Letter*. An unbiased, independent poll conducted by Gallup in May and June

2014 revealed that 63% of consumers are *not* influenced by social media regarding their buying choices and only 5% claim that social media has a significant impact on their buying decisions.

"63% of consumers are not influenced by
social media regarding their buying choices"

Dan says that given the loud and relentless drum-beating about everything you MUST engage in, do, and involve your business in, in social media, you'd think it'd be like 95% being influenced. Now he does say there is a legitimate *defensive* need for many businesses to be present and accounted for in the social media places and it's still possible to utilize it for direct, accountable, profitable lead generation or drive to purchases.

But that 5% statistic speaks very loudly to Dan and to him it says, "Beware the hype. Do NOT fall victim to the false idea that social media has replaced other, much more reliable and essential advertising and marketing media. Do NOT feel like some sort of failure if you can't seem to get business by using it. Do NOT risk diverting time, energy or resources away from proven media that works for you to chase this unicorn—it can only be added and experimented with, not embraced as a suitable replacement."

So back to our question—How's one to keep up with it all? How can you maximize the potential positive impact that social media can have with the tremendous "time suck" it can become for many people? Certainly a key factor is recognizing the appropriate use of each of the social media platforms.

We've talked earlier in this book about the importance of truly recognizing who your target market is. Each social media platform has its own unique demographics and, depending on who your target market is, should have an impact on how you divide up your social media efforts. Take a look at these interesting statistics from BusinessInsider.com:

- 86% of Facebook's users are outside the U.S.
- 68% of Instagram's users are women
- Google+ users are 70% male
- 84% of Pinterest users are female

So, for example, if you're writing a book about football it wouldn't seem to make much sense to apply a great deal of social media effort to Instagram or Pinterest compared with other platforms based on the statistics above.

Certainly you need to have an awareness of the various platforms and their associated demographics to determine where you should concentrate your efforts. Our good friend Mary Agnes Antonopoulos (MaryAgnes.com) recommends you not be on every social network. She suggests you pick two to focus your efforts on in order to build an audience, convert clients and build your brand.

Mary Agnes is certainly one of the resources we'd recommend you check out if you're looking for training or assistance with your social media. Another great resource is Carol McManus, who you can find out more about at LinkedInLady.com. Both ladies know their stuff and if you decide that handling your social media marketing efforts is not one of the hats you want to be wearing they can get you pointed in the right direction.

One thing that both ladies highly recommend is that you tie your social media efforts together to maximize your time. Take advantage of tools that exist that allow you to leverage your time across multiple social media platforms. If you "tweet" something via Twitter can you have it automatically appears as a Facebook post? You can.

But you do need to be careful of certain things when you automate posting material to your social media networks. Using social media automation tools can help you maintain a consistent social media presence without sacrificing the rest of your work. Here are some dos and don'ts primarily related to Twitter from VerticalResponse.com on how to integrate social media automation into your online marketing.

#1 Do mix up your automated tweets and status updates with ones you write in real time

#2 Don't automate messages during inappropriate moments

#3 Don't only post your own thoughts and material

#4 Do test out multiple platforms for their capabilities

#5 Do use platforms to monitor or listen to what's going on around you

#6 Don't use Twitter simply to curate work by importing RSS feeds from other blogs

#7 Do maintain a consistent voice

#8 Don't post too often

#9 Do schedule tweets for promotions or events in advance

#10 Don't tweet posts once and then forget about them

A few simple Google searches can uncover the appropriate do's and don't for the other social media platforms as well. Smart authors recognize that social media should play a part in their marketing efforts, but only you can determine how large of a role it should play. It can definitely become a big time sucker and Dan Kennedy recommends that you give it its due, but don't credit it with more than it really deserves.

Dan says that bottom-line: no one can argue against the popularity of social media, or it's engaging and consuming the time of a large segment of the population. But smart marketers who can do math can and do question its influence on consumer' buying behavior. So should you.

Lack of a Press Kit

One of the most powerful ways to build your platform is to leverage the power of the media to help you spread your message. That being said, the media whether it be online, print or broadcast media, is inundated with information every single day. They're busy—they've got deadlines to meet and it's a real struggle to get noticed in today's world.

You want to be noticed by the media. And there is a lot of media out there. You've got magazines, trade publications, newspapers, book reviewers, book bloggers, talk radio, broadcast and cable TV and more. It is your job as an author to make it easy for the media to work with you.

The single most important element you need for the media is what is called a Press Kit or Media Kit. Today, press kits are primarily digital in nature and available online although it doesn't hurt to have a few physical copies available also. Online locations for your press kit can include your website, your book website and your blog.

Your press or media page on your site(s) is where you'll want to direct inquiries about your book. You'll want to have lots of information available for those busy reviewers, researchers, editors, reporters and others so they can easily find what they need.

So what are the key elements of a media kit for a book author?

Reviewers will expect to find certain things in your online press kit. These include:

- Your author bio which should include other books you've written and your qualifications for writing this particular book
- Press release
- Your photograph
- Photograph of your book

There are other items that you might add to your press kit, but remember that more information is not always the best thing to do if you want your message to be noticed. Other possible additions might include:

- A sample review—great for reviewers with time constraint
- Sample chapter from your book
- Ready to use interview questions
- Specific information about your book
- Testimonials from early readers with authority or celebrity

You don't want to hide your press kit on your website. Make it easy to find. It should be included in your main page navigation so site visitors can quickly locate it. Most often, the documents will be in the form of a PDF or Zip file that is downloadable right from your site. We recommend PDF because a zipped file requires the potential reviewer to go through more steps to view your info and we're all about making it as easy as possible.

"Don't hide your press kit on your website"

Here are links to some sample media pages for various authors so you can see what others have done and model their success.

- Seth Godin—http://www.thedominoproject.com/press
- Dr. Marty Rossman—http://worrysolution.com/press-kit/
- Michael Hyatt—http://michaelhyatt.com/platform/media
- Joel Friedlander—http://www.thebookdesigner.com/companion/media-kit/

Here are some additional details about some of the elements you might include in your press kit.

Author Bio

We recommend you have both a long version and a shorter version of your author bio. At the least, the first two paragraphs of your longer author bio should be able to stand on their own. A typical author bio is around 200 words and it should make you stand out from the crowd. Don't forget to include your contact information including phone and email along with social media links.

What makes you stand out from the crowd? What's your "hook?" Maybe it is other books you've written, maybe it is your education, maybe it's some interesting experiences you've had while traveling. You want to be interesting and unique. But be yourself. It's important to be authentic.

Press Release

Your press release should be no more than a single page and should focus on the launch of your new book. Be sure to include info that makes you and your book newsworthy. Be sure to not include information that is time sensitive (such as an upcoming live event) so your press release and media kit remain evergreen as much as possible.

Photographs

For any photographs you should have both low resolution versions (72 dpi) for online use as well as higher resolution (minimum 300 dpi) for use in print. You can't grab an image of a website and expect it to look good in print. It won't.

Ready to Use Interview Questions

Remember, you want to make it as easy as possible for a prospective interviewer to work with you. If you think they're going to take the time to read your book from cover to cover in order to come up with a great list of potential questions you're kidding yourself. So prepare in advance a list of possible interview questions (and responses) about yourself and about your book.

This might include questions about what inspired you to write your book, your background or upcoming projects. This section of your press kit is especially helpful for those extra busy bloggers and interviewers who would love to help you promote your book but don't want to start with a blank piece of paper.

Specific Information on Your Book

According to Wikipedia about 2,200,000 new books were published last year. That's like 42,308 new books every week of the year. No wonder it's so hard to stand out from the crowd. So in this section you need to talk about what makes your book different. You need to describe your book in relation to the features that make it unique.

Why did you write it? Was there a hole in the marketplace for your type of book? Did all the others books similar to yours lack some critical piece for which you provide the solution. You need to convince the person who will be reading your press kit that your book is a story that will be interesting for their audience.

Contact Details

Make sure your contact information is easily available to your site visitors. If a potential reviewer likes what you have they may want to get in touch with you for a follow up. Provide contact information that looks professional. Nothing makes you look smaller than using a gmail or AOL type email address. It screams "Mom and Pop" operation. Be sure you have an address like press@YourAuthorWebsite.com.

Remember, your press kit doesn't have to be overly complicated. Keep your format and your font usage simple. If you're putting together your first press kit you probably already have some of the materials you'll need. Don't be overwhelmed. Just begin with the items you already have and then build the rest piece by piece. Do not wait until the last minute, when your book is ready to launch, to throw together a press kit. Be ready for the media.

> Free video training from Rick Frishman on book publicity available at Author101Online.com

Mistake #35

Lack of a Blog

There seems to be an ongoing debate out there as to whether blogging is really beneficial for authors in today's social media marketing world. Let's cut right to the chase—if you're an author you need to be blogging.

Why? Here are four major reasons you need to be blogging:

#1 Your blog is a great way to drive traffic to your website

#2 Adding fresh content to your blog can dramatically improve your search engine optimization

#3 Your blog related to the subject of your book positions you as a leading authority

#4 Your blog is a fantastic way to develop deeper reader (or prospective reader) relationships

Driving Traffic

Your blog provides you an opportunity to create relevant content for your potential readers. Use this as a marketing tactic to drive traffic back to your primary website. Many recommend that your blog be the focal point for all of your social media platforms.

Yes, you're still going to have your Facebook, Pinterest, Twitter, LinkedIn, YouTube and Google Plus presences. Use all of them to post relevant visuals of your blog articles. Give your social media followers a reason to click through to your website. Be sure to post inbound links directly in your blog articles in order to drive traffic to specific landing pages within your website.

Search Engine Optimization

Fresh content is still king in beating out your competitors in the search engine results page. By using appropriate keywords in your articles you can dramatically improve your search engine optimization. Take some time to list out the keywords, topics and categories you'd want people to use to find your blog. Be sure to use these words and related expressions when writing your blog posts.

"Fresh content on your blog is important
for obtaining better search engine results"

Keywords and keyword phrases on your website are a significant way in which Google (and other search engines) find your site for these searched words.

Become a Leading Authority

Well-written articles position you as an authority in your niche. By posting articles which resonate with your potential readership you show the market your knowledge and strengthen your position as someone to which people should pay attention.

You're building trust. The more you can show that you're well-versed on your topic, the more likely your potential readers will hang on your every word and likely purchase your book and recommend you to their friends and colleagues.

Developing Deeper Reader Relationships

Blogs provide another means to deepen the connection with your readers. By connecting directly via your website, your readers are able to get to know you better and you greatly improve that all important know, like and trust factor. You build trust by being a source of information. Readers like to be informed, and appreciate that you are the one teaching them.

Additionally, just as you would on your various social sites, respond to comments and interact with your followers. If they have questions about your topic or the book you are writing, respond to them directly on your blog. Unlike many social media sites, your blog is generally searchable on your site for quite some time. Your website comments last far longer than any Twitter response or Facebook post. Other potential readers will see your interactions too.

There are some additional benefits from regular blogging that many people don't consider. First, it's a great way to become a better writer. The only way you become a better writer is to write, and the regular posting of articles to your blog forces you to write regularly. The more you blog, the more you write, the better writer you become.

And, if you're a first time author, you need to remember that the publishing business has changed drastically over the last few years. If you're hoping to get noticed by a publisher they're far more likely to pay attention to you if you have a built-in audience of readers. And that's where your blog comes into play. So blogging is not just a great way to become a better writer, it may be your quickest route to becoming a published author.

Blogging is also a great way to get quick feedback on an idea you may want to develop further. While traditional authors may have to wait months between finishing a book and reading the reviews, a blogger gets to read their readers' comments the same day that make a blog post. Having additional outside perspectives and the occasional constructive criticism can be invaluable.

Bloggers usually spend the majority of their time sharing their insights and ideas with their readers. But, if you're willing to listen, you'll find that your readers share a lot with you too. Knowledge of your audience is invaluable. Achievement of this type of insight is a natural result of your day-to-day routine as a blogger.

There's no question that becoming a regular blogger requires a commitment of time. But you've got to remember that blog posts can be pre-scheduled, so it's okay to write things in advance and schedule them for release at a later date. We highly encourage you to do this. Take a day or two and focus dedicated effort to the pre-writing of your blog posts for the next year. Stay ahead of the game as much as possible so you don't have that dreaded "I've got to write another post" hanging over your head day after day after day.

How often should you post to your blog? Some advocate doing a daily post, but in our opinion two to three per week is plenty. At a minimum, be sure to post some new content weekly. And, if your content well seems to be running dry and you're struggling with what to write a blog post about, check out John Kremer's excellent blog post titled "*Book Promotion Tip: 101 Ways to Blog as a Book Author*" on his site at blog.bookmarket.com

Blogging is still very important for authors. So be sure to commit yourself to being a blogger to help you increase your platform.

> Check out the Mistakes Authors Make blog
> at MistakesAuthorsMake.com/blog

Mistake #36

Not Attending Live Events to Network

ere's a list of well-known information marketers—Alex Mandossian, Armand Morin, Wendy Lipton-Dibner, Jim Edwards, Perry Marshall, Ryan Deiss, Sean Roach, Michael Penland, Christina Hills, Mike Filsaime, Stu McLaren, Michel Fortin, Jeanette Cates, Alexandria Brown, Brett McFall, Ted Ciuba, Tom Hua, Joe Polish, John Assaraf, Joel Bauer, Connie Green and Ray Edwards.

What's common about them all aside from the fact that they are Internet/information marketers and we've been blessed at Speaker Fulfillment Services to be able to work with all of them? They're all people that we first met in person at a live event.

Yes, you can establish great relationships online. But the people who you will become closest to and who will be most willing to help you build your platform as an author are those people who you've had a chance to meet face to face and establish a personal relationship with.

"The people you will become closest to and who
will be most willing to help you with your book
are people you'll meet face to face at a live event"

Your best joint venture partners, super affiliates, clients, etc. will come from the group of people who you've taken the time to get to know by being where they are. You can build a publishing empire on your own. But it's a lot easier if you have relationships with the movers and shakers in the industry and the places you get to know these people are at live events.

If you're not attending two to three live events each year we believe you're truly stunting the growth of your publishing business. Rick's *Author 101 University* is a must attend. Aside from the fantastic training you'll receive from the best in the industry about what's working and not working in the book-marketing world, you'll have an opportunity to meet with those movers and shakers. Literary agents are in abundance and it's a great chance to pitch your ideas and get great feedback.

Check out the next *Author 101 University* at http://Author101.com.

There are other excellent events geared for authors. Our friend Judith Briles puts on an annual event called *Author U* that Bret has spoken at multiple times. For more info visit AuthorU.org. There are also a myriad of Writer's Conferences that focus more on the actual writing process plus additional book marketing and publishing related events you can attend. A simple Google search can uncover any number of possible events that you can become involved with.

Now don't get carried away. There's a time for learning and networking and a time for doing. If you become a seminar junkie who never takes the time to apply anything you've learned, then all the relationships you've forged will be of no value.

So how do you get the most out of a live event?

There are three distinct phases to any event you're going to attend—Before, During and After.

Before the Event

First, determine what your goals are for attending a particular conference. Is it to meet certain people or to find potential affiliates or joint venture partners? Maybe it's to find an agent or a publisher or talk with a vendor at the show that can be a resource. Maybe it's just to nurture existing relationships. Whatever your purpose, or purposes, clarify them in advance of the event.

Come prepared with some business cards, copies of your book (if it's done) and something to take notes in. You meet a lot of people at events. If you don't jot a quick note down after a conversation about who you met, what you discussed and what your follow up will be they all blend together very quickly

Familiarize yourself with the speakers and what they'll be talking about. You should attend as many sessions as you're able to attend, as you just don't know when that idea will hit you upside the head that will benefit you. If the event offers multiple simultaneous learning tracks determine who you're going to listen to ahead of time.

At the Event

Remember that you're not alone. Most people are not comfortable walking into a roomful of strangers. You've got to be able to step outside your comfort zone because networking at events can help you grow your business. Learning to mingle and to follow-up with contacts you met at a conference is crucial to your long-term success as an author.

Don't spend time at an event only with those people you already know. Move around and get to meet as many people as possible. Approach things from the mindset of "What can I do for you" rather than from the mindset of what you can get from others. It's about the relationship.

When you meet a new person shake his or her hand and repeat their name. This not only helps you remember the name, but it also shows you're making an effort to hear the name properly. Wear your nametag on your right shoulder so people can easily see it when they shake your hand.

Be sure you craft and practice a short description of yourself and your book that can be said in 30 seconds or less. This is what's known in industry as your "Elevator Speech."

Listen more than you talk. Nothing is as flattering as someone who listens carefully and shows sincere interest in other people. Ask questions and listen to the responses so you begin to understand the person. This will help you to identify who might be a potential affiliate, JV partner, mentor or other possible resource for you as an author.

As mentioned before, take notes to help you remember what people have said. When you get back to your office, put all this information into your contact management software.

After the Event

Once you have someone's business card, make sure you follow up with them as soon as possible after the conference. If there is an obvious win-win connection with someone you've met at an event, reach out to them to explore a possible collaboration further.

Bret and Bryan always reach out in writing with a simple hand-written note to any contacts they've made at an event. These can be new contacts or people who they've met previously. You'd be amazed at the tremendous response a simple hand-written note receives from the person it was sent to—because most people rarely receive them.

Immediately after an event has concluded you need to create your post event action plan. Of course you have people you need to follow up with and that should be near the top of your list. But you may have specific tasks you need to do as a result of something you learned. You may have on-going training you need to work into your schedule. You may have vendors you need to follow up with to advance things forward. Whatever it is, the key phrase here is "Prioritize to Maximize." You're invariably going to have a lot of things to do right after an event so make sure you manage your time wisely.

Conferences present a wonderful opportunity to meet new people and begin the establishment of relationships that can further your platform as an author. Take advantage of them!

> Join us at the next Author 101 University.
> Use coupon code "MAM" to save half off your tuition.
> details on the next event can be found at Author101.com

Not Owning Some Key Web Properties

S ocial media is just one key component of your online marketing strategy. Another aspect is your own web properties and there are at least two that you must own.

The first is the .com of your name. So, if your name is Andy Author you want to own the domain AndyAuthor.com. Your name domain should be the portal to everything you. People should be able to access information about you and be able to find links to all your books and other products from this site.

But, if you have a common name and that domain is already taken you'll still want to get a .com address rather than one of the other extensions such as .org, .net, .biz or something else. Why? Because people always think of .com first and foremost.

So if your name is already taken as a .com domain you have a few options.

#1 Your name with "The" in front of it. e.g. TheRickFrishman. com

#2 Your name including your middle initial included. e.g. BryanEHane.com

#3 Your name followed by the word "Author". e.g. BretRidgwayAuthor.com

The second property you should own is the title of your book.com. So, for example, the domain for this book would be MistakesAuthorsMake.com. We talk more about book titles elsewhere but Rick flatly states that if you don't own the .com of your book title then it isn't your book title.

"If you can't get the .com domain for your book title then it isn't your book title"

.Com addresses are less than $10 per year. Now, a few words of warning here. Don't get too carried away with the purchase of domain names. We've all had lots of great ideas and gone out and grabbed domain names for that idea and then had the domain sit unused for year after year after year. Even at only $10 a pop it starts to add up, especially if you're not using the domain.

> A great source for domain names is
> Rick's own RicksCheapDomains.com

Your AuthorName.com URL should appear in many places. You never know who might pick up a piece of literature about you and want more information. It could even be a representative of the media. So make it easy for people to find you. Here are just few places you'll want to include your website URL:

- Business cards
- Sales flyers
- Bookmarks
- On cover and inside of your books
- Thank you cards
- Letters
- On packaging of other products of yours
- Email signature files
- On banners if you exhibit at events

Be sure that on your website and on your book title website that your contact information is very easy to locate. Nothing is more frustrating than going to a website and not being able to find out how to contact someone. You'll need to decide if you want to have people contact you via email or phone, just be sure whichever you choose that the necessary info is easily located on your site(s).

Here's a few other Do's and Don't related to your websites from Bret Ridgway and Frank Deardurff's book *"50 Biggest Website Mistakes: Secrets to Getting More Traffic, Converting More Customers & Making More Sales."*

- **Do** keep your key information above the fold. For example, if you have an optin box on your home page make sure your site visitor doesn't have to scroll down to find it.
- **Do** make sure you test your website in different browsers. What looks great in Firefox might look terrible in Chrome. Make sure your site looks good for all major browsers.
- **Do** be consistent with your branding. Your book title website should have a similar look and feel as your book cover.
- **Don't** get crazy with fonts on your website. Too many font types makes it difficult to read your text

- **Don't** make your site a nightmare to navigate. Keep it as simple as possible.
- **Do** make sure your ordering process is straightforward. If people can order your book or other products on your site make sure you fully test your shopping cart and make sure the look of your checkout page is consistent with the branding of the rest of your site.
- **Don't** do a text only website. Use video, audio and other modalities to more fully engage your visitors
- **Don't** use outdated photos of yourself on your site. You want someone who meets you at an event to actually recognize you.

We highly encourage you to utilize WordPress as the foundation of your website. While you probably don't want to build your own websites from scratch, by having them built in WordPress you'll have the ability to easily add more content to your site whenever you want. Webmasters can be pricey and if you have to wait on someone else to make even minor changes to your site it can become very frustrating. Almost everyone uses WordPress these days and you should too.

According to WordPress more than 17% of the web is powered by WordPress—a figure that rises every day. Everything from simple websites, to blogs, to complex portals, to enterprise websites and even applications are built with WordPress. WordPress sites are also extremely search engine friendly, as there are plugins that automatically take care of 80-90% of the mechanics of search engine optimization for you. And being found on the Internet is obviously very important to you as an author.

Best of all, WordPress is a free platform and you can have the look customized for you by the use of what are called "themes." There are literally thousands of different themes available from which you can choose. So you no longer need to learn HTML or CSS to do websites (unless, of course, you want to). But it's probably not one of those hats you should be wearing.

There's no doubt that your web presence is a very important part of your platform as an author. Make sure you give much forethought to how your websites are going to fit into your total marketing mix and that you build things in a logical manner. You'll come out ahead in the long run when you do.

To avoid other critical mistakes authors make with their website check out Bret Ridgway and Frank Deardurff's book *50 Biggest Website Mistakes Online Business Owners Make* at 50BiggestWebsiteMistakes.com

> Free training video on Internet marketing
> for authors by Author 101 University
> instructor Peggy McColl available at
> Author101Online.com

Understanding How One Achieves Bestseller Status

You hear it all the time in the book world—that magic word "bestseller." We're all pretty familiar with the *New York Times* Bestseller List and Amazon bestesellers. But did you know there are also all of the following bestseller lists?

- ABA IndieBound
- Barnes & Noble
- Publishers Weekly
- The Boston Globe
- USA Today
- The Denver Post
- The Wall Street Journal
- The Los Angeles Times

- WalMart.com
- BN.com

It's a very confusing world, with all these different bestseller lists. Each has its own criteria on how you make their list and it's easy to get lost. It is certainly a credibility enhancer as an author to be able to say you're a bestselling author. And, regardless of which bestseller list you're on, there is a big difference between being an author and being a bestselling author. But what does that really mean in the scheme of things?

We're not going to cover the criteria associated with every bestseller list here. Let's focus on the two biggies that most people are familiar with—the *New York Times* and Amazon. Of these two the *New York Times* list is far more coveted by authors and, correspondingly, far more difficult to achieve.

The metrics the *New York Times* uses to determine their bestsellers is different than the metrics Amazon and others use. Publishers know the *New York Times* gathers its book sales data from a selected few bookstores such as Nielsen's and that it does not take into account the actual sales of the books such as Amazon does. Rather, it looks at how many books were shipped to these particular stores in anticipation of sales.

The *New York Times* list heavily counts sales in its selected brick-and-mortar stores. As a result, if your book isn't in those particular bookstores then your chances of making the *New York Times* bestseller list is very, very small. You've got also to remember that Amazon carries ten times or more titles than your typical average bookstore.

It's only within the last couple years that the *New York Times* even started counting online sales along with books that are in the brick-and-mortar stores. According to certain publishers and other industry insiders, it takes somewhere around 20,000 books ordered during a week at these select bookstores to have a chance at the *New York Times* bestseller list. If you are lucky you know which bookstores. Most of us aren't privy to that information however.

Another important difference between the *New York Times* and Amazon is in their timing. The *New York Times* compiles their list based on a week's performance of a book, while the Amazon list is compiled by the hour. And Amazon has a lot more categories in which one can become a bestseller than does the *New York Times*. So that begs the question—does being on Amazon's bestsellers list actually mean you're selling more books than being on the *New York Times* list?

In some instances the answer is yes. It comes down to *Actual Sales (Amazon) vs. Anticipated Sales from Select Bookstores (New York Times)*. It's still wonderful and highly prestigious to be known as a *New York Times* bestselling author, but it doesn't mean that authors on other bestselling lists are not bestselling authors as well. It just means that your book did not ship enough or fast enough to one of the specific bookstores that the *New York Times* pulls their data from. Bottom line, the *New York Times* list is not always the most reliable indicator of actual book sales.

Amazon is the world in which authors have a bit more control over when it comes to making their bestseller lists. Whether you're trying for the top 10 or even the top 100 the most important thing you can do on Amazon to make this happen is….

Focus all your sales into one day.

Amazon keeps their exact formula secret for picking their top books, but it's obvious that how many books you sell in a short period of time weighs mightily into their results. Less sales on a single given day will drive you higher up their list than the sales of more books spread out over a longer period of time.

Don't try to game the system. If you buy 500 copies of your own book you won't hit the Amazon bestseller list. If you have your brother buy 500 copies of your book you won't hit the bestseller list. Amazon tracks IP addresses, credit cards, and more to make sure authors aren't

200 | **MISTAKES AUTHORS MAKE**

trying to buy their way onto the list. In their world a bulk sale for any number of a copy of a book counts just as one sale. Your best strategy is to build your list and then get your followers to buy your book all at the same time.

On your launch day on Amazon you typically need to make 500 sales in order to make the top 100 in a given category. To make the top 10 you need to generate 2000 sales of your book.

"On your book launch day on Amazon you typically need 500 sales to make the top 100 in your category"

We know authors who have invested hundreds of thousands of dollars in order to make a bestseller list. In some cases it paid off, as the profit they generated from the back end products and services they offered through their book more than covered their upfront investment.

But in some cases we know it didn't really pay off in the long run. They may have become a bestselling author but they lost money in the process because the entire business around their book wasn't in place yet.

There are outside organizations authors can hire to help them achieve bestseller status. Some of them cost in the hundreds of thousands of dollars. If you've got a big bankroll and getting on that bestseller list is that important to you than go for it. It's your call.

There's certainly a certain cachet still to being able to say you're a bestselling author. But it's even nicer to know you're a profitable bestselling author.

Mistake #39

You Can Write a Book but You Can't Write Sales Copy

We've talked extensively through this book about how the real work begins once you've actually got your book written. Now you've got to market your masterpiece and that can be a very intimidating thought for many people.

While you're writing your book you are often in a "zone" and the words flow from your fingertips almost effortlessly, like water from a spigot. Then you need a different kind of writing—copywriting—and you simply freeze up. The words don't flow. Maybe because now you have to put on your sales hat and talk about your book in a different way and it just doesn't come naturally to you.

Copywriting—the art of writing sales copy—is a skillset all to itself. When we talked earlier in the book about the many different hats you're going to have to wear copywriting wasn't even mentioned. But it should have been there. Why? Because your copywriting skills (or those of someone you outsource this to) will be needed for many different things in the marketing of your book. This could include:

- Sales copy for your book website
- Script for a book trailer
- Descriptions for Amazon and other distribution channels
- Your book title
- Your book subtitle
- Printed sales literature
- Autoresponder messages
- And more

Copywriting is definitely one of those skills it is highly valuable to possess and, as an author, most of us are able to tackle this task ourselves. But if you decide that it is one of those tasks you want to outsource to someone else then, at the least, you need to have a good understanding of what makes for good sales copy, as you will be reviewing anything someone is writing on your behalf about your book.

We're probably all familiar with the terms features and benefits as it relates to sales copy. Features are the facts about something. For example, your book is 172 pages in length. That's a feature. Or it's 8-1/2" x 5" in size. That's a feature. Or it's printed in 12 point Palatino font. That's a feature.

"You've got to describe the benefit of the benefit"

A benefit is the result that the reading of your book will bring to the reader—more money, more time, lose weight. But, more importantly and often overlooked, is the benefit of the benefit. What will making more money bring the reader—the ability to lie on the beach and drink margaritas? What will losing weight mean to the reader—the ability to attract and marry the mate of their dreams? You've got to think beyond the direct benefit in many cases and paint a picture in the minds of the reader of your sales copy the end result they'll receive from reading your book.

There are several different schools of thought on the best way to approach the copywriting process. If you're serious about mastering this craft then study the methods of outstanding copywriters like John Carlton, Ray Edwards, Gary Bencivenga, Michel Fortin, Lorrie Morgan-Ferrero, Bob Bly and David Garfinkel. All of them know how to write copy that sells.

A while back Bret interviewed another noted copywriter, Alex Mandossian, and Alex espouses two major copywriting styles—the John E. Kennedy model and the Dale Carnegie model.

John E. Kennedy lived about 100 years ago. He was a Canadian Mountie and probably the first copywriter to be a millionaire of all time. Here's his formula. There are three parts to it.

1. Make a clear promise. Make the promise clear, and hit 'em right between the eyes. It could be the first sentence, it could be the headline, but make a clear promise.
2. Give reason-why proof. You make a promise, and then you've got to prove it. Reason-why proof is using the word 'because.' For example—'You know, I'm going to let you save $100 if you purchase this, because I have no testimonials, and I just want to promise that you'll give me a testimonial, and I'll let you save 100 bucks from it.' You know? —as a reciprocity motion on my part. Don't give an empty promise.

    The biggest mistake most copywriters make is that they don't prove the promise. They just make the promise because they know that they have to make it, but they don't give good reasons why. And the magic word is 'because.' You can say almost anything after 'because,' and it becomes memorable and convincing.

3. The third step is simple: the Call to Action. You make a promise, you give reasons why (you're proving that promise), and then, get them to do something. Order now, click this link, call me, get a free consultation, opt in to three free chapters—whatever. Make the Call to Action clear, so that people actually do it.

Now, the second type of copywriting model or philosophy is Dale Carnegie's. I don't hear anyone talking about this, but he also has a three-part model:

1. Tell a memorable story. People love stories. Number 1 because they usually happened; and they like to fantasize about fables. Kids love stories; I think that's where it comes from: 'Once upon a time…' We're born and we grow up with stories. They're memorable because they have a beginning, a middle, and an end, a tip and a tail. It's easy to repeat a story, and I think it's memory that makes stories so powerful. So, give a memorable story.

2. Carnegie says the second step is Give the Call to Action. Give the call to action after telling a story. 'So that's why I want you to…' and tell them what to do. 'Now that you know this, I want you to buy the book.' 'Now that you've heard the story, I want you to go out and get this mining equipment.' 'Now that you've heard this story, I want you to get this video set.' Okay?

3. Then, what Carnegie does, the third step, is give the benefits that they will gain by taking that action.

Both methods can be highly effective and Alex stated which he uses depends upon the situation. In his autoresponder messages he loves the

Dale Carnegie model. He'll start with a memorable story that someone can sink their teeth into, and it doesn't look like the typical autoresponder message. In other situations the John E. Kennedy method will fit better.

Which method should you utilize? The answer is it depends. It depends on what the use of the copy will be. It depends on what writing style with which you're most familiar and comfortable. There is no right or wrong answer.

Study those copywriters mentioned earlier. The ability to write good sales copy is a skill any author should possess. And check out the resources section of this book for our recommended list of copywriting books that should be part of any serious copywriter's library.

> For some of the greatest books on copywriting
> ever written visit MarketingClassics.com

MARKETING YOUR BOOK AFTER IT'S WRITTEN

Not Using Public Speaking to Build Your Platform

The reason many people are not using public speaking to grow their book platform is because they are afraid of public speaking and, as a result, avoid it at all costs. If you like to speak, or even if you are willing to speak, you will find it a highly effective way to more quickly build your book platform. You can attract new clients, build your email list and gain new opportunities. When you deliver a speech it is as if you are having an introductory phone call or an initial appointment with a whole room full of potential book buyers all at once.

Here are some of the top reasons why you will want to get on board the speaking bandwagon:

Become Recognized As an Expert In Your Niche

When your name is on the event brochure and you're standing in the front of a room speaking on your topic, the audience assumes you're an expert on that topic. The more potential clients think you are an expert, the more likely they are to want to buy your book and other products and services that you may have to offer. You become known as an expert in your field and people will refer people to you when someone they know needs what you have to offer. Why? Because being a speaker on a topic positions you as a sought after expert.

Meet More People More Quickly

People do business with people they know, like and trust. Speaking gives a group of people an opportunity to get to know you all at once. When anyone in your audience needs your book or other services you can provide they will be more likely to call you because they have already met you and have begun to "know, like, trust" you because they received value from your presentation.

Create New Opportunities

Speaking will allow you to go before groups of people that you may not otherwise meet. This can help you expand your sphere of influence, build your permission-based email list and provide you with a variety of new opportunities. The more people you deliver a speech to, the more opportunities for additional speeches, writing and being a guest on radio and television shows will come your way.

Meet Other Experts and Leaders

Speaking allows you to meet other successful people in your industry. One day you may find yourself on the platform with the person you admire most. What could be better than that? Always be gracious and generous with your time and acknowledge others for their accomplishments and their presentation. The other people you meet on the platform can be great referral sources and strategic alliance partners for you in your business.

More Clients, Contracts and Commissions

Speaking can be far more cost effective than advertising, direct mail, networking or cold calling. The rate of return on the time investment you make to prepare for and deliver a speech could turn out to be the smartest action you could do to generate new business. If you have a strong delivery and give a high content speech, you could leave a speech with at least one new client every time you speak. Sometimes you could come home with ten or twenty new clients, which sure makes for a good day of speaking.

Increased Visibility

Whenever you are in the front of a room speaking to a group, you are being noticed. People will remember who you are and what your business does. The more people see you and see your business name, the more successful people think you are. Often, when you speak to a group, the group publicizes the event.

Many people who do not attend the event will still read the information about your business and may give you a call. Even if people do not call you, know that the more people who read your name and see your picture the more they feel comfortable with you and begin to trust you for future business dealings.

Keeps You in Touch with the Public

Speaking keeps you in touch and on your toes. It allows you to discover what issues are of concern to the people in your audiences. Then you can address these concerns in your articles, videos, blogs and on your website. Also, when you get out of your office and connect with new people they ask you questions or your opinion on topics you many have not yet thought to address. This can also result in new products, services and revenue streams for your company.

It is Good for Your Own Personal and Professional Growth

When you go to different groups, meetings and conferences as a guest speaker you will have many opportunities to hear other presenters on a variety of topics. Not only will this expand your network—you will learn a lot while keeping current on a variety of topics. This is always energizing and you may come home with an idea that will transform your business and uplift your life.

Build a Better List, Better and Faster

When you go to speak to a group, the people in that group have a positive experience of you and you are beginning to build a relationship with them. When you do a drawing or offer them a discount if they give you their email address you are building your list. This is one of the key objectives you have as a business owner. You always want to be building your list.

The people on your list who have had a personal experience with you through your speech are more likely to be your book buyers sooner than someone who signs up and joins your email list through your website, but has never met you or seen you present.

More Money Later

Many people will be impressed with you when you speak and they may be interested in what you have to offer. By you staying in touch with them via email you will find that some people will come back to you later when they need what you offer.

"Becoming a public speaker is probably the single best way to help you build your book platform"

If you want to really build your book platform becoming a public speaker is probably the single best way to help you do that. Never underestimate the value of being the one in the front of the room. The instant credibility it provides you is immensely powerful and makes overcoming any fears you may have about public speaking well worth it.

Need some help brushing up your presentation skills?
Our good friend Wendy Lipton-Dibner offers
some fantastic training on how to do just that.
Check it out at MovePeopleToAction.com.

Mistake #41

Becoming a Media Diva

Let's get real folks—you need the media a whole lot more than the media needs you. So when you have the opportunity as an author to be in front of the media first and foremost, be grateful. Be sure to thank your interviewer right away and then following up with a personalized, hand-written thank you note after an interview goes a long way.

Will an interviewer read your book before an interview? Probably not. Don't get upset if they don't and don't get upset if they get some facts wrong along the way during your interview. Never make them look bad or stupid or you'll probably blow your chances for future media coverage. What show host wants to bring on a guest they've seen treat previous hosts poorly? None.

Never ask for a "do over" of an interview. Most media people simply don't have the time. Just learn from your mistakes and strive to do a better job the next time out. The best thing you can do with the media is build relationships. Show up on time, be prepared and don't forget to show your gratitude for the time you're given.

You want to be a show guest who creates an extraordinary experience for that show's audience. Anything you can do to make your host look smart, savvy and like a superstar is well worthwhile. You want to do more than just "give a speech." Become a go to guest that show producers and hosts can count on.

"You want to be a show guest who creates
an extraordinary experience for a show's audience"

Be the show guest who is available at a moment's notice to step in and fill a seat if someone else has to drop out at the last minute. But be careful that you strike the proper balance during any interview. Your publisher may be telling you to "Push the book—push the book—push the book—you are there to sell." Well, yes and no.

Often authors are trying to sell their book so hard that they turn off the host and the audience. There is a quid pro quo here. The host will introduce you as the author of your book in the beginning. Then maybe in the middle of the interview—and hopefully once at the end.

That's great! You want him to promote your book—not you. But if you keep talking about it you will come off as a pushy pain in the butt author—and you don't want that. Your job is to teach the audience—make them fall in love with you. Not to just sell your book.

There are three words you NEVER want to say in an interview. The 3 words you NEVER say in an interview are "In my book." You can refer to it by using the title ... e.g. "When I was researching '*Where's Your Wow'*—I interviewed 100 CEOs and they taught me that..."

A couple of more tips for an interview:

Over-prepare for your interview. Keep in mind that your job is to share your information and deliver an entertaining and informative interview. To begin, it's important, even if you only have a minute, to successfully interact with the host. When you greet him or her, be sure to pronounce your name. Say, "Hello, I'm Rick Frishman. I'm the coauthor of the Author 101 series." This will increase the odds that your name is pronounced correctly and that the host knows that you wrote your book.

Immediately thank the host for having you on, and, if you watch the show regularly, say so. "Jill. You're a credit to television. I have been your fan since you started on the morning news." Create a connection.

Similarly, if you should have an opportunity to speak at a conference be sure that you are someone who is easy to work with. I've been to events where a speaker was so demanding that they literally drove the event promoter nuts. They had to have green M & Ms in a glass bowl on stage, a very specific brand of bottled water, etc., etc., etc. They were not invited back to that event again.

If you're an author who has an opportunity to speak be the speaker who is available before your presentation and always after your session. It greatly adds to the positive experience attendees have at an event when they can meet the speaker, ask questions, shake hands, pose for a photo, sign books or autographs and visit one-on-one. An exceptional speaker thinks of themselves as a co-host of the event and acts accordingly. This really enhances the attendee experience.

Don't be what is known in the industry as the "hit and run" speaker. We have all seen them—this is the guy or gal who shows up a few minutes before their speech and disappears shortly after their speech has ended—never to be seen again at the event. It leaves a sour taste in the mouths of the attendees and does not ingratiate you with the event promoter.

Courtesy is always foremost, and speakers need to be able to handle all situations with grace, flexibility and professionalism. It is important that you, as the speaker, show warmth and be generous with everyone.

Do not believe what it says on your speaker marketing materials about you being world renowned—today you are the hired help. Do not act like a diva, act like a gracious professional.

There will be times when something unexpected happens that is potentially detrimental to your performance on the platform. How you handle yourself when things don't go as expected says a lot about you as a person and how you choose to handle yourself will be noticed by both the event promoter and the audience. Want to kill your future speaking opportunities? Just act like an ass when the going gets bad and you can just about guarantee your failure.

A smart speaker offers, with the event promoter's permission, during their talk to send an ebook, valuable list or an audio download that supports the talk to the audience after the talk is over. Even offer to be available for any calls and emails.

Stay in touch with audience members who want to hear from you and continue to offer value. This can be a free report, fact sheet, ebook, articles, blog entries and video clips—anything that adds value to the presentation. This type of activity also communicates your ongoing interest in providing value to the group and demonstrates your commitment to serving the group for the long term.

The way you over deliver as a speaker ensures you create raving fans. When you make your meeting planner's or event promoter's job easier and you make them look good you will be invited back every time.

Public appearances, whether on television or radio or at a live event can dramatically help you build your platform as an author. Be attentive to your host's needs and deliver a first class experience for their audience every time. Don't be a diva.

Mistake #42

Not Being Ready for the "Big Stage"

While we said in the previous chapter that you need the media more than the media needs you there are those that would argue the opposite. John Kremer, author of "*1001 Ways to Market Your Books*," claims the media needs you more than you need them. They have so many hours of air time to fill that they are continually in search mode for new and interesting guests.

So, the question is, are you ready to be that new and interesting guest? When the lights shine brightly are you ready to take center stage and deliver a powerful and impactful few minutes that will cause people to really stand up and take notice of you. Not everybody is ready for the limelight but, if you're serious about building your platform as an author, you need to be ready.

We advise that you don't go for the big stages from the get-go. The *20/20s*, *The Today Show*, and the *Good Morning America*s of the world are all wonderful vehicles for gathering massive exposure. But, if you're not prepared to be on the big stage, and you totally bomb on your appearance then you can dramatically impact negatively your chances of future media appearances.

"You should 'cut your teeth' on local media first"

You should "cut your teeth" on local media first. The morning or mid-day news shows typically have a segment where a local person is brought on to talk about some subject. You still want to be prepared for these types of appearances but better to learn from your mistakes on a smaller stage first before tackling the big boys.

But whether it's the local media or the national stage what are the best things you can do to prepare yourself to have as positive of an impact as possible? You need to look good on video and, if you're serious about becoming really good on video, you'll want to give thought to getting some media training to help you create the best impression possible.

Keep in mind that looking good on video goes beyond television appearances. You should have your own YouTube channel where people can check you out. You need to look as good in your YouTube videos as you during any live appearance on television.

Our good friend Starley Murray of StarleyMurray.com offers some excellent media training and if you think media training is on your "need to do" list then check out her services at StarleyMurray.com. According to Starley, here are the 7 top things you need to do to make sure you're ready before you appear with the media.

Promoting your book in television media and social media is an exciting and sometimes overwhelming process. For most authors the intent is to share their message, to sell their book and share themselves with the viewing audience.

One of the most common mistakes is approaching the situation thinking only about what you want. First think about what others want out of this exchange for media coverage and media viewing.

Think of your two groups of people. First is your target market and how you can best serve them, second is the producer or media decision maker who is making it possible for you to be seen and heard by your target market. Luckily, both usually want the same thing from you.

In the next seven steps you will learn what is most important to those you are intending to serve and share your message with. At the same time, you will notice that what you want is probably already covered in what they want. If it is not covered, likely it can be easily layered into a publicity strategy to serve everyone's needs.

Often when I ask my author coaching clients what they think they need to be media ready, they list the THREE following areas:

a) Know how to LOOK on camera
b) How to SOUND on camera
c) Know what their MESSAGE should be

These three primary ingredients are a great start. We are creating a seven layer cake that everyone loves and will taste great with every bite. Each of the ingredients work together for an enjoyable experience.

Now let's layer on top of LOOK, SOUND & MESSAGE with what your target market and media decision makers want, need and frankly demand of you to be MEDIA READY.

#1 Are You Easy to Understand and Do You Have a Unique Brand?

Often in the quest to be creative and fun we can become confusing. If you had to pick the lesser of the evils... it's better to be clear and boring that exciting and confusing. Plan how you can stand out in a crowd and showcase your individuality.

#2 Do You Understand What Polished Appearance Means?

Most of us think our appearance is limited to our body, face and wardrobe. It's amazing how distracted audiences can get judging makeup and hair styles due to the extreme styling built into the business. However, do not forget that your body language, facial expressions and props are all part of your polished camera image.

#3 What Does It Mean to Be Entertaining?

You do not have to be a professional comedian or entertainer to hold an audience's attention. If your subject matter is exciting and your delivery is authentic and energetic you are heading in the right direction. Telling short relevant stories can help you connect with your audience.

#4 What are the Expectations to Best Educate?

You are the expert at what you write about so your audience expects you to share not easily known facts. They are looking for the scoop and they are used to receiving it in a short, concise and easy to understand delivery. Audiences love stats, facts and visual aids.

#5 How Do You Hold Energy With No Dead Air Time?

You may think that a YouTube video or television appearance three minute segment is short. However, you may discover this is a sprint to the finish line, multi-tasking several objectives often leaving you dead air while you are thinking of your next thought. Rehearsal is key even if you are a natural on camera in order to stay within segment deadlines.

#6 How Do You Have a Conversation and Avoid a Sales Presentation?

Some of the most popular authors and industry experts come across natural on camera because they are actually being themselves and having a conversation instead of a presentation. Do not ever lose your authenticity if you receive professional media training. It is connected directly to your integrity and protects your expert message.

#7 Provide Social Proof With Video!

To give you an edge over most authors who are pitching to get on television, create a three minute mock interview video. Not only can you use this for your pitch but you can also use it on your website, YouTube channel and possibly your information products as part of a book sales bundle.

Bonus: Consumer Alert

Oh, and by the way the number one complaint of the thousands of TV producers I've worked with is that the guest expert did not research the show format, audience, look and feel of the show. How can you be media ready when you don't know what the media wants from you?

Luckily, there are a ton of free tips on the Internet about how to be media ready. Most are awesome. However my advice is to consider who the source is making the recommendations as there is no certification for this expertise.

The majority of media trainers are retired by as much as two decades from live television and are also not current with their own social media or creation of YouTube videos. Follow those who are active and with experience.

It's easy to out check experts and easy to execute the above tips that are the current standards and are in support of your success.

Congratulations on investing in yourself to become media ready!
Great advice and our thanks to Starley for sharing.

Without a doubt many people approach media interviews from
the wrong mindset. If you're an author and a media appearance awaits
don't treat it as a challenge, some ordeal to get through as unscathed as
possible. Your goal is not to just avoid saying something stupid or just
'sound good.'

You need to view every media appearance as an opportunity to
get your key message out. Keep in mind that it might not only be a
television appearance. Maybe some journalist who's up against a tight
deadline needs your help via phone. Be prepared to make the most of
the opportunity.

So how do you make the most of your opportunity? Here are some
important things to keep in mind when you prepare for an interview:

- Take some time to do a little research in advance. Find out
  what you can about the interviewer and the program you'll be
  appearing on.
- Make sure you know how long your segment is supposed to be.
  There's a big difference between a 30 second sound bite and a
  4-5 minute piece.
- Know in advance the three key points you want to make.
  Practice—practice—practice the best way to get your points
  across.
- Make sure during an interview you treat every question as an
  opportunity to articulate one of your three key points. That
  doesn't mean you don't answer their question. You can do that
  also, but don't lose sight of the fact you have something you
  want to say.
- Gently try and take control of the interview. Don't be aggressive.
  Answer questions in a manner that allows you to say what you

want. A phrase such as 'I think the point to remember here is...' is a perfectly good way of answering a question during an interview and steering things toward your three major points.

- Show confidence. TV interviewers are generally good at putting you on your back foot. The entire broadcast environment can be intimidating. Remember, you will always know more about your subject than the interviewer. There's nothing wrong with correcting a factual inaccuracy in a question to establish you as the expert. Just correct it... gently.

- Stick to your agenda. Although you may be tempted to venture into other areas that aren't your strength it will generally lead you into trouble. And it's also a big time waste because it's keeping you from the main topics you wanted to cover.

- Try to enjoy your experience and make sure you learn from it. Be sure you review your performance so you can see how to improve for your next media appearance.

Free training video on Maximizing Television and Video for authors by Author 101 University instructor Starley Murray available at Author101Online.com

Mistake #43

Underestimating the Power of Radio

Alex Carroll is the undisputed expert on how to use radio to sell more books. We highly recommend his materials and, in fact, you can even get a free list of the top 20 nationally syndicated radio talk shows just by opting in at his site RadioPublicity. com. He even gives you their addresses, phone numbers, and the names of both the hosts and the producers. Shows that reach 75 million people.

According to Alex, more than 200 million American commuters listen to the radio on their way back and forth from work every day and that radio stations need more than 10,000 guests per day to fill up their shows with interesting and enlightening content. Alex says "If you have something to talk about they need YOU!

Can you save people money? Save them time? Make them rich? Tell them an amazing story? Make them laugh? Teach them something new? Get them arguing about a controversial topic? Enrich their lives?" It's a win-win situation. You give the radio show great programming…they give you great promotion.

And Alex should know. He's been a guest on radio shows, at last count, 1,264 times! He's received over 4-1/2 million dollars in free airtime that has resulted in over $1,526,000 in direct sales of his book about how to beat speeding tickets.

Here are just a few of the benefits, per Alex, of using radio publicity to sell more books:

- You get to advertise for free as radio interviews cost nothing.
- You can do radio interviews from any phone, anytime, anywhere
- You'll often get an entire hour or more of free airtime per interview
- You'll become recognized as the expert on your subject
- You'll have a captive audience of thousands… even millions… of listeners
- Your list of fans, friends and e-mail subscribers could explode

According to Mark Victor Hansen and Jack Canfield, coauthors of the *Chicken Soup for the Soul* series, radio interviews were the primary driver of helping them to sell over 100 million books. It's hard to argue with success like that.

If you were buying radio time Alex says that you can expect to spend a few hundred dollars per minute at a minimum for mediocre stations up to $30,000 per minute for major nationally syndicated shows. As a beginning author few have that kind of budget so that's why radio publicity is so important.

According to a recent survey by Statistical Research Inc., 96% of the US population listens to the radio at least once a week and 75% listen EVERY DAY… more than any other media.

And interview time is worth more than ad time. Why? Because people pay more attention to the shows than the ads…and they're much more likely to believe them. Think about it. Which do *you* pay more attention to? The commercials or the guests?

They key to success with radio is to focus on the larger shows. It's fine to "cut your teeth" on local media till you've got your presentation down pat, but to really move larger quantities of your book you must focus your efforts on those programs that have massive reach. It's not about the power of their broadcast signal; it's about the number of actual listeners.

"The key to success with radio is to focus on the larger shows"

Does it take some work to get yourself booked on radio shows? Of course it does. You'll need to develop a good media kit. Initially, you'll probably want to do most of the calls yourself working from a list of the best stations you'll get from Alex or another source. But getting booked on radio shows is another one of those "hats" you'll be wearing so you'll have to decide at some point in time if you want to enlist other people to help you in reaching out to the radio shows.

When you are booked on a show be sure to capture the following critical information:

- Station's call sign letters
- City where the station is located
- Name of the show
- Host's name
- What time zone station is located in
- What time your appearance is scheduled
- How long your appearance is to last

Always try to get an mp3 file of your interview on the station. You'll want to post your interview on your website unless, of course, it's terrible. In that case listen to it repeatedly so you can learn from your mistakes and do a better job the next time out.

A lot of what we discuss in this book about not becoming a media diva applies equally well to radio appearances as it does to television appearances. You need to be flexible, you need to be available on short notice and you need to express gratitude to the show hosts and producers who put you on their program. The handwritten thank you note goes over just as well with this crowd as it does with the television crowd.

Make sure you know who is calling whom. Are you calling into the show or are they calling you? Most will initiate the interview call. Due to the cost of international calls it's always a good practice to have out-of-country interviews call you. And, if possible, take interviews on a landline rather than on a cell phone.

Make sure you have a quiet environment in which to conduct any phone interview. Honking cars, crying babies and other noise distractions do not lend themselves to a high quality radio spot.

Be sure to smile when you say "hello." While a smile is a visual cue, it also tightens the muscles in your face and throat, lifting your voice just a tad. Studies show that people can actually hear that smile.

Remember, by and large, most radio hosts are not interested in talking to you about your book. What they want to hear about is the news that your book ties into or expands on, and your take on it. You can ask to mention your book in the initial booking conversation. Some will not allow it, some will.

What will usually happen is that the interviewer will state your name and your book at the beginning and end of the interview. Some will also state your name and book coming out of, and going into a commercial if you are on longer than 10 minutes.

Try and find a local angle. You will be more interesting to a show's listeners if you can give them some sort of local tie-in. Not to mention that you'll also be more likely to land the interview in the first place.

If your interview is cut short after a few minutes of a planned half an hour interview you may need to work on your skills. Go back and listen to the interview to find out how you can improve.

Like any marketing effort, it takes a commitment and perseverance to achieve the highest levels of success. Radio publicity is no exception. But your ability to reach thousands of people all at once for an investment primarily of just your time can pay massive dividends.

> Recommended Resource
> Alex Carroll's RadioPublicity.com

Mistake #44

Not Leveraging the Full Power of Amazon

Without a doubt the 800-pound gorilla in the book-marketing world is Amazon. More books, both print and ebooks, are sold on Amazon by far than by any other channel. Amazon is a very polarizing entity; as there are many that hate what Amazon has done to the publishing industry and others who love what all Amazon has done for them.

For example, we operate an online bookstore at SFSBookstore. com that sells many hard-to-find books related to copywriting and advertising. The site has been online for probably well over ten years. Yet, we easily sell ten times as many books via our Amazon presence as we do through our own site.

The question for you is how can you best leverage the full power of Amazon to help you take your publishing success to the next level? Amazon offers so many different services it can get quite confusing quite quickly. So let's first try to get the lay of the land and gain an understanding of some of the key Amazon services available for authors.

Author Central—At Author Central, you can share the most up-to-date information about yourself and your works with millions of readers. You can add your biography, photos, blog, video, and tour events to the Author Page, which is your homepage on Amazon.com. It's essentially your home page on Amazon.

You can see timely sales data for free, including sales trends over time and where in the US your books are selling.

Kindle Direct Publishing—Kindle books are hot—hot—hot and as an author you should definitely be making your books available for the Kindle platform. While the sales price for Kindle books is usually pretty low (99 cents to 2.99 in most cases), ebook sales are growing rapidly and having Kindle products is a great way to more quickly build a following for your writing.

Many have discovered the greatest value with Kindle is to crank out short books (often less than 50 pages) on very specific topic to use as lead generators for their other books, courses and other products and services.

Many well-known marketers, including our good friends Tom Antion, Daniel Hall and Jim Edwards offer excellent training on how to get the most from Kindle publishing. Check them out. There are many authors who claim they are making six figure incomes selling nothing but inexpensive Kindle books.

CreateSpace—Amazon's service for self-publishing of paperback books. Printing is on-demand, so Amazon only prints up a copy of your book when you've received an order they need to fulfill. So you don't have to maintain any inventory.

Amazon charges you a fee for signing up for the program, a varied percentage depending on whether you're selling through the CreateSpace bookstore or the Amazon bookstore (20% to 40%), plus the cost of printing your book which is based on your page count

It's very important to analyze your total costs to determine if CreateSpace is right for you. While the convenience of having no inventory is wonderful, if you clear only a couple dollars on each sale after all of CreateSpace's fees are accounted for then you may want to give it more thought.

A lot of it depends on what your goal for you book is. If it's all about maximum revenue generation from book sales that's one thing. If it's about getting your book in as many hands as possible because your real profit will be in the conversion of readers to higher end products and/or services then your actual profit per book sold may be less of a concern.

Surprisingly, Bret and Bryan's core company, Speaker Fulfillment Services (SFS), has a number of clients who order their books in quantity from CreateSpace in fairly low volume, ship them to SFS who then fulfills individual orders directly to end customers for sales made via the client's own website. Thus they gain the benefit of an almost print-on-demand scenario where they maintain very low inventory levels that enable quick order fulfillment for their own website orders.

ACX—First, confirm that you hold the audio rights to your book. If you do then it may be worthwhile to check out the Audiobook Creation Exchange (ACX), where you can bring your book to life in audio. Amazon says you can earn royalties up to 90% and you'll be able to distribute your audiobook through Audible.com, Amazon.com, iTunes and more

Amazon Advantage—Amazon Advantage works like a consignment store. Your books appear on Amazon.com as a product sold by Amazon. You don't need to fill your garage with copies of your books waiting to be sold, and when you make a sale, you don't have to wrap and ship the book. Amazon Advantage does it. Books you sell on Amazon.

236 | MISTAKES AUTHORS MAKE

com through Amazon Advantage are eligible for their free super saver shipping and two day shipping through their Amazon Prime™ program.

Here's how it works. Amazon places orders with you or your fulfillment house for copies of your books based on customer demand and you (or your fulfillment house) sends them the copies. Amazon stores them in their fulfillment centers, and when a book is sold, Amazon handles the payments, wraps and ships your books, and takes care of customer service and returns for you. Amazon pays you monthly for the books they sell. Naturally, there are requirements, so be sure to check out the full details online.

Amazon Advantage is not intended for resellers or sellers of used books. If this is your situation, instead of Advantage, you should consider Selling on Amazon and possibly Fulfillment by Amazon.

Selling on Amazon—Like Amazon Advantage, when you use Selling on Amazon, you can promote and sell your books direct on Amazon.com and use the Amazon fulfillment network to store, package, ship, and service your orders. Unlike Amazon Advantage, Selling on Amazon is like having your own small store on Amazon. com. Your products are listed and appear on the Amazon.com website as sold by you. In other words, you are listed as the "seller of record" and receive payment and feedback for your orders, but without needing a merchant account.

You pay a commission on the sale price of the item and other selling fees (the commission for selling a book is a flat $1.20 plus 15% of the item cost). At the time of publication of this book the cost to be a Pro Merchant on Selling on Amazon is a $39.95 per month subscription fee. Or, you can be an Individual Seller and pay $0.99 per item sold (with no monthly commitment).

Fulfillment by Amazon—If you desire you have the option of Amazon being your fulfillment house. If you include Fulfillment by Amazon with your Selling on Amazon account there are also storage, packing, and shipping fees. Fees vary by the size, weight, and price of the item. For example, a 2-pound book that was priced over $25 would cost $1.80 for fulfillment and about $0.05 per month to store. Storage fees vary by size.

The world of Amazon is a complex one. Be sure to fully study any potential Amazon service in depth before deciding which, if any, are a fit for you. Make sure you know all the costs and restrictions associated with any program before diving in.

"One of the most overlooked benefits of Amazon is its value as a research tool for authors"

One of the most overlooked benefits of Amazon is its value as a research tool for authors. People coming to Amazon are buyers—they're looking to purchase a book or other product. Whereas, people going to Google are generally searching for free information. So how can you use Amazon as a research tool?

#1 Find The Best Selling Books in Your Niche—Amazon itself has its Amazon Best Sellers Data that gives complete information on the best sellers of each item, best-selling items, most gifted items and most wished for items, based on each category and even sub—category

#2 Study Your Competitors—Titles and description are the two important factors that captures the attention of your customers. You can check out your competitor's book titles and descriptions as a model for writing your listings. You can check out how others in your niche are pricing their books and see what color schemes and cover layouts are working best.

#3 Conduct detailed Keyword Research—Once you know which books are bestsellers, and who are your competitors, your next step is to empower your listings and titles. Conduct detailed keyword research to find out what people search on.

Not Getting the Most out of Book Signings

The thought of doing a book signing will send many authors heading to the hills. They imagine sitting all alone at a table, hour after hour, just hoping that someone will come up and buy their book. And that investment of several hours of time in exchange for selling just a handful of books seems counterproductive at best.

With the massive decrease in the number of brick and mortar bookstores these days the role in person book signings plays in the marketing mix for most authors has decreased dramatically. And rightfully so. But that doesn't mean that, should an opportunity for a book signing arise, you should automatically reject the idea of participating.

With any marketing endeavor you've got to decide what your objectives for undertaking that marketing task are. It could be as simple as selling "x" number of books. But if you keep it as simplistic as that for book signings you can be overlooking some significant secondary benefits you maybe never even considered. Of course, selling some books is probably your primary objective. Most authors report they sell anywhere from 5 to 100 books at most book signings. But, like any marketing effort, you typically get out of it what you put into it. And book signings are no exception.

You should promote your book signing through the local media yourself and you should also enlist the assistance of your local bookstore in helping you promote your book signing. If you can tie in any local radio or television appearances with your book signing by all means do so.

Do you have an email list of fans of yours that you've built up through your online efforts? Segment that list by city or zip code and invite those that live near to where your book signing will be happening to come by. It's always nice to have some folks who already appreciate your work come by and help talk you up to others in the bookstore. Ask them to bring their friends by to your signing. And, for those of your fans that don't live in the area of your book signing, maybe they have friends that do.

Take full advantage of your social media platforms to spread the word about your event. Post it on Facebook, Tweet it to your followers and put it on your website.

With bookstores you'll need to be proactive throughout the process. Your first call to a store will be to set up your book signing but expect to make several follow-up calls to make sure they're ordered your book and that they are also promoting the signing. You need to make sure you're on their calendar.

Always be asking if there is anything you can do to help. You can be apologetic for contacting them frequently, but don't worry about being too sorry—your book signing is helping them get more business.

If you're taking books yourself to your signing you'll need to be in contact with your publisher or book printer directly if you're self-published to make sure your books are on the way to the bookstore. Don't assume that once you've mentioned it to the publisher or printer it's done. Follow up with them also to make sure all the details have been suitably handled.

You should dress what is called "business casual" for a signing. No one wants to watch a sweaty author squirm around in an uncomfortable suit all day long. Make sure you bring yourself something to drink as you'll find you'll need to wet your whistle frequently if you're talking throughout the day.

Some other helpful items for a more professional signing would include:

- Business cards, especially if you have back end products and services to your book.
- Lots of pens. Blue ink is preferred as it appears more personable than black ink.
- Any promotional items you want to share.
- Blowup of your book cover (Visit PostUpStand.com) for some cool mini pop-up banners.

Be prepared for the unprepared bookstore. You might also have a tablecloth of your own you can use just in case and things like tape and markers to make your own signs if the bookstore is clueless.

"Be prepared for the unprepared bookstore"

If you're a natural introvert you'll need to put on your game face and become more extroverted at a book signing. Don't be afraid to smile and to greet customers in the store. Invite them to check out your books. Worst thing that can happen is they say no. Next!

If you don't have a lot of experience with book signings then go to other book signings. Take a look at how other authors are interacting with the public. See what type of promotional materials they're using. Think carefully about what made you aware of that book signing and consider that in relation to your next book signing.

Here's our good friend SuzyQ's (SuzyQCoaching.com) Top 10 List for Book Events

1. Always smile.
2. Always carry a Sharpie.
3. Dress for success.
4. Be approachable.
5. Take photos.
6. Be engaging.
7. Emphasize your unique branding.
8. Relax, be authentic.
9. Turn fans into your personal sales force.
10. Have fun.

You'll notice that SuzyQ's list was titled "Top 10 List for Book Events." A book signing would certainly qualify as a book event. But one of the most overlooked and underutilized marketing avenues to build awareness for you as an author and for your book(s) is to combine a book signing with some type of workshop.

Maybe the bookstore you're considering for a signing event has a meeting room that you can use for anywhere from two to four hours to actually teach something related to your book. Then, at the end, you sell your book to the attendees. Or maybe they pay a fee to attend the training workshop and receive your book as part of their tuition.

Many local public libraries also have meeting rooms you can reserve for trainings. Obviously you'll need to make sure it's okay to sell your book at the end as you want to abide by their rules for meeting room use.

Bottom line is a book signing doesn't have to be just a book signing. Maybe it can be more.

You may remember we mentioned earlier secondary benefits to book signings aside from book sales? If you're trying to build your platform as an author one of the things we discussed earlier was the importance of using public speaking to help build that platform. Every book signing is a mini public speaking opportunity. The more comfortable you get in front of a crowd of strangers the better you'll become at public speaking. Use your book signings as a confidence booster in relation to public speaking.

Book signings still have a place in today's book world. Just be sure you leverage them as best as possible for maximum benefit.

Incomplete Profile Pages in Your Distribution Channels

We talk elsewhere in this book about some key web properties you should own as an author. First was your book title and the second was your name. On both sites you're going to have information about yourself—your bio, your photo, listing of all your books, etc.

But these are not the only places where you need to have information about yourself as an author. You need to be where the book buyers are which is, first and foremost, Amazon.com. Amazon and other online distribution channels typically offer their authors what are called "Profile Pages" where you can tell their audience more about yourself. Amazon calls theirs Author Central.

As an example here is the beginning section of Rick Frishman's Author Profile page on Amazon:

Rick Frishman	
	Rick Frishman, publisher at Morgan James Publishing in New York and founder of Planned Television Arts (now called Media Connect), has been one of the leading book publicists in America for over 36 years. Rick works with many of the top book editors, literary agents, and publishers in America, including Simon and Schuster, Random House, Wiley, Harper Collins, Pocket Books, Penguin Group, and Hyperion Books. He has worked with bestselling authors such as Mitch Albom, Bill Moyers, Stephen King, Caroline Kennedy, Howard Stern, President Jimmy Carter, Mark Victor Hansen, Nelson DeMille, John Grisham, Hugh Downs, Henry Kissinger, Jack Canfield, Alan Deshowitz, Arnold Palmer, and Harvey Mackay. Morgan James Publishing publishes fiction and nonfiction books by authors with a platform who believe in giving back. Morgan James gives a portion of every book sold to Habitat for Humanity. Rick has… Read more

To get a look at Rick's complete profile just go to Amazon.com and type "Rick Frishman" into their search box. "Amazon's Rick Frishman Page" usually comes up near the top of the listings in the search results. You'll notice in the complete profile a listing of all of

Rick's books sold on Amazon as well as links to his most recent tweets and blog posts.

So why is it so important to take advantage of your author profile pages on Amazon and on other sites that afford you that opportunity? A well put together profile page provides you an opportunity to establish your credentials as an expert in your niche by providing specific information about your background and links to your presence elsewhere on the web—your social media sites, etc.

Profile pages are a valuable part of painting an online picture of your expertise for not only the social networks, but also for search engines and other information aggregators. A good profile page allows you to expand your presence and increase the interaction you have with your readers.

"A good profile page allows you to expand your presence and increase the interaction you have with your readers"

Key elements of a well-designed author profile page include:

- Your real, full and usual name
- Links to your articles
- Your biography with links relevant to your expertise
- Your contact information
- Your picture or avatar (be sure to use a current picture)
- Social media account links

If you're wary of unleashing the spam monster by making your email address available to readers then you can utilize a contact form as an alternative.

You'll want to be sure to keep your information current on the various sites on which you have profiles. For example, Amazon's Author

Central has an "Events" section where you can post information about upcoming events at which you'll be attending. Maybe it's a book signing or maybe it's a conference at which you'll be speaking. Take full advantage of the opportunity to share with the world where they can find you.

Make sure you keep good records of all the sites on which you have profiles. If you write another book you'll need to go back to all of them to make sure your new title appears in the list of books which you've authored.

Your readers want to know more about you. Obviously, it's your choice as to how much information you want to share. But if you're trying to build your platform as an author and/or speaker then you should be very willing to share more information about yourself to help you achieve that know, like and trust factor that you're looking for as an author.

You'll want to share your Author Page URL that you create, for example, in Amazon Author Central via your email signature, your blog posts, your Facebook posts, your Tweets and more. Your web presence should be an intermingled spider web of sorts where there are many different ways people can find you and enter your world.

And don't hesitate to utilize automated tools like HootSuite that allow you to preschedule your tweets for release at specific times. Blog posts can also be prescheduled so you don't have to worry every week about getting some new content out there for your readership.

You'll also want to be sure that you maintain a consistency across the various profiles sites and social media platforms with your naming conventions. If your author profile page is under the name Rick Frishman, for example, then you'll want your Facebook profile page to be Facebook.com/RickFrishman and your Twitter profile to be Twitter.com/RickFrishman. Consistency will help you in your branding efforts and make it easier for people to find you online.

As much as possible you'll want to link your various accounts together so you don't have to manually update everything one at a time whenever there is something new to report. You can link recent blog posts and tweets right into your Amazon Author Central page. You can tie RSS feeds to things so that whenever you post a new article it automatically is pulled into your profile. Automation is a wonderful thing.

Failure to utilize the author profile pages that are available to you at no cost (yes, they're free) is wasting a marketing opportunity. You need to be out there in as many places as possible where your readers and potential readers can find you. Take full advantage of them.

Mistake #47

Underestimating the Value of Book Reviews

t's well known in the marketing world that what others say about you carries far more weight than what you say about yourself. And, in the book world, what others say about your book carries far more weight than what you say about your book. What others say about your book is usually in the form of a book review and having them (especially, good ones) can really pump up your marketing efforts considerably.

Most people these days are familiar with Amazon book reviews. Many reviews are by friends and family of the author and these so-called "amateur reviews" certainly carry some weight and the more positive reviews you can muster the better. But Amazon also has what are known as professional reviewers. They rank their reviewers and even have a Reviewer's Hall of Fame.

It is considered highly valuable to get one of Amazon's Top Customer Reviewers to give you a book review. But we've got to say it can be a real challenge to find the proper reviewers to submit your book to. There are 10,000 customer reviewers listed on Amazon's reviewers' page at http://www.amazon.com/review/top-reviewers. You have to click on each individual reviewer's profile to find out what types of products they review. Many just review electronics and other consumer items, so finding ones who review books in your niche isn't easy the first time around.

Make sure you keep a good list of those people you identify who are suitable to request a review from so the next time around you won't need to start from scratch. One way you can possibly shorten this process is to look at reviews of other books in your niche and see if any of those reviewers of those books are on Amazon's Top Customer Reviewers list.

The soft-sell approach typically works the best with Amazon's Top Reviewers. Simply offer them a complimentary copy of your book in return for their considering it for review—no obligation. Be sure to carefully screen out reviewers whose profile indicates they wouldn't be interested in your book.

Only a small percentage of the reviewers you approach are likely to respond. That's okay. They're busy people who are regular recipients of review copies from publishers who already have their mailing addresses and who are already familiar with their reading preferences.

Another way you can distribute complimentary review copies of your book is by taking advantage of book social-networking sites. The two most popular are Goodreads.com and LibraryThing.com. At LibraryThing you'll sign up as a "LibraryThing Author" and then you'll participate in the "member giveaway." Be sure to request gently that they also post their review on Amazon. Some reviewers are more than happy to do it for you.

Don't just limit yourself to Amazon reviewers though. Take a look at any trade publications serving your niche. They're an excellent possible source for a book review. You've also find other good potential reviewers in:

- Colleagues and other acquaintances interested in the topic of your book
- Influential bloggers who write on your area of expertise
- Local press who like to highlight local authors
- Active participants in forums and discussion boards about your topic

Never ask for a review from someone who hasn't actually read your book—even if it's your own mother. What you'll end up with as a review that seems unconvincing and that will detract from your book's credibility, rather than add to it.

"Never ask for a review from someone who hasn't actually read your book – even if it's your own mother"

Be sure to acknowledge with a personal hand-written note anyone who has given your book a review. As mentioned before, you may gently ask them to post their review on Amazon.

Don't be afraid to give away a few books. The potential loss of a few sales will be more than offset by the positive word of mouth exposure you should receive. Readers who enjoy your book will tell their friends and colleagues about it.

Although we all consider it perfectly ethical to ask for reviews, never do anything to suggest that you're expecting favorable treatment. If you succeed in getting a lot of reviews, you can anticipate that somewhere along the way there will be some negative ones.

You can possibly protect yourself by asking a Top Reviewer to not post their review of your book if they simply hate your book. But

254 | MISTAKES AUTHORS MAKE

it's there call entirely. In some cases, reviewers are willing to give you prepublication feedback that might provide you with valuable advice on fixing your book's weaknesses. But don't expect that and, of course, never ask for it.

You may simply want to avoid sending your book to reviewers who usually post harshly negative reviews, but don't shy away from those who offer frank criticism. While positive reviews can certainly help your book negative reviews on Amazon might have a bigger impact.

A recent study by the Yale School of Management reported that multiple over the top glowing reviews for a book tend to be dismissed by potential book buyers as hype generated by you, the author, or by your publisher. Negative reviews are actually taken more seriously since buyers usually believe they represent honest criticism from disappointed readers.

For a much more detailed look at book reviews we highly recommend Dan Poynter's book *The Self-Publishing Manual*. In the 14th edition I have in front of me it's in chapter 7 on Promoting Your Book. I'm sure Dan has come out with a more recent edition since then.

Dan's got a ton of great resources, contact lists and other information that will prove immensely valuable to you when you're considering your marketing approach to review copies of your book. You can pick up more info on Dan's resources on his site ParaPub.com

The secrets to getting the most from your book reviews is to get the real "movers and shakers" in your niche to review your book. Malcolm Gladwell discusses in his popular book *The Tipping Point* about the importance of identifying those real centers of influence that can have massive sway over the market. Positive sway if they get on your side and negative sway if they don't.

Not Capturing the Browsing Buyer

What do we mean by the browsing buyer? We mean the person who's either in a physical bookstore or online at Amazon.com or BarnesAndNoble.com who is looking for a new book to buy but they don't have a specific author or title in mind. So they're browsing the shelves in your brick and mortar bookstore or they're typing in keywords online searching for that next book to be their perfect reading adventure.

We've already talked about the importance of a great book cover and a great book title, both of which are critically important to getting noticed when someone is browsing those bookstore shelves.

In that environment your book might be one of a few dozen or a few hundred at the most in your particular niche. So a great cover and title can definitely get you noticed by that browsing buyer. But what about in the online bookstores where your book is just one of hundreds of thousands or millions of books? How can you have even a chance of getting noticed online?

What if you have a book on improving relationships? A search this morning on Amazon.com for the keyword phrase "relationships" returned 297,400 results. Your book isn't a needle in a haystack. It's the tip of a needle in a haystack online.

How about if your book is about coaching?" You've got a better chance there. Your book is only one out of 26,785 results that came back for the phrase "coaching." Now maybe you're at least the whole needle.

Here are just a few others to give you a better idea of what you're up against:

Success books—202,792
Love books—468,817
Self-Improvement—69,220

You get the idea. It's hard to stand out in an overly crowded marketplace. So what's one to do to increase your chances of getting noticed by the browsing buyer online?

Certainly the higher you can get in the results pages Amazon or Barnes and Noble displays when a potential buyer types in their search term into the search box the better it is for you. So how do you do that?

Here are Amazon's own suggestions on this topic:

"To increase your book's discoverability on Amazon, you need descriptions and keywords that accurately portray your book's content and use the words customers will use when they search. Along with factors like sales history and Amazon Best Sellers Rank, relevant keywords can boost your placement in search results on Amazon.com. Best practices with keywords:

- Combine keywords in the most logical order: Customers will search for military science fiction but not for fiction science military.

- Use up to seven keywords or short phrases. Separate them with commas, and keep an eye on the character limit in the text field.
- Experiment. Before you publish, search for your book's title and keywords on Amazon. If you get irrelevant results, or results you dislike, consider making some changes—your book will ultimately appear among similar results. When you search, look at the suggestions that appear in the Search field drop down.
- Think like your customer. Think about how you would search for your book if you were a customer, and ask others to suggest keywords they'd search on.

Do not include these things in keywords:

- Information covered elsewhere in your book's metadata—title, contributor(s), category, etc.
- Subjective claims about quality (e.g. "best")
- Statements that are only temporarily true ("new," "on sale," "available now")
- Information common to most items in the category ("book")

Common misspellings:

- Variants of spacing, punctuation, capitalization, and pluralization (both "80GB" and "80 GB", "computer" and "computers", etc.). The only exception is for words translated in more than one way, like "Mao Zedong" and "Mao Tse-tung," or "Hanukkah" and "Chanukah."
- Anything misrepresentative, such as the name of an author that is not associated with your book. This type of information

can create a confusing customer experience and Kindle Direct Publishing has a zero tolerance policy for metadata that is meant to advertise, promote or mislead.

Don't use quotation marks in search terms: Single words work better than phrases—and specific words work better than general words. If you enter "complex suspenseful whodunit," only people who type all of those words will find your book. You'll get better results if you enter this: complex suspenseful whodunit. Customers can search on any of those words and find your book.

Other metadata tips:

- Customers are more likely to skim past long titles (over 60 characters)
- Focus your book's description on the book's content
- Your keywords can capture useful, relevant information that won't fit in your title and description (setting, character, plot, theme, etc.)
- You can change keywords and descriptions as often as you like
- If your book is available in different formats (physical, audio) keep your keywords and description consistent across formats
- Make sure your book's metadata adheres to KDP's Metadata Guidelines."

Obviously these suggested guidelines come from their Kindle Direct Publishing wing but the same concepts apply to non ebooks also on their site.

More important than your keywords and the other metadata for your book is the categories and sub-categories you list it in when you're putting up your Amazon listing. At last check Amazon allowed you to choose 5 categories for Kindle books but only 2 categories for physical books. Go figure.

Your selection of your categories and sub-categories within Amazon can have a massive impact on how likely the browsing buyer is to find your book. And once you've set your categories for your book within Amazon *you're stuck with it*, so give it a lot of thought and do research before you make your category selections.

"Your selection of categories and sub-categories in Amazon can have a massive impact on how well people find your book"

The number of books you need to compete against to be noticed in your category influences heavily how high you might appear in the results. A Google search for some case studies related to the number of listings returned from minor tweaks in how category listings are done will be very insightful and we'd encourage you to do it.

An excellent article that will help you save time understanding the importance of how you categorize your book on Amazon can be found in our resources section at MistakesAuthorsMake.com/resources under "Additional Reading."

Getting noticed by the browsing buyer is a big key to achieving greater publishing success. Of course you'll have your own followers who will buy anything you write. But it's the getting noticed by the people who might not be aware of you in advance that can take you to the next level.

No Use of Video in Your Marketing Efforts

We talked earlier about being ready for the big stage. We briefly mentioned YouTube and spoke about how you want to look as good in any YouTube video as you would on a live set. But YouTube is such a potential marketing powerhouse for any author that it is worthy of a deeper look.

Quick quiz—name the three top social networks you're asked to go visit for additional information at the end of television commercials? Most can name Facebook and Twitter easily, but how many of us would name YouTube as the third player in the group? You should.

YouTube is the world's second largest search engine behind its parent company Google. YouTube has over a billion (yes, billion with a "b") active users every month. At last report more than 6 billion hours of YouTube content was being viewed by people every month.

That's an average of almost one hour per person for every single person on the plant.

"YouTube is the world's 2nd largest search engine"

Every brand, and yes you Mr. or Mrs. or Ms. Author are a brand, should have your own YouTube channel. You simply can't deny the incredible marketing power that is YouTube.

With Facebook and Twitter we all collect followers and engage with them by creating content. Eventually, we look to turn that relationship into more than just pure content, as we begin to market to those users at some point in the future.

It turns out the same approach works as well as or better on YouTube. If you consistently create content and share it with your followers your brand can grow. And the beauty of it all is that, unlike the transitory nature of Facebook posts and Twitter tweets, your YouTube videos have unlimited shelf life.

The key with YouTube, as it is with any marketing channel, is consistency. As an author if you can put out regular content that is consistent with your branding that is optimized to get your target audience viewing.

So what are some of the keys to getting the most out of YouTube? YouTube Search Engine Optimization (SEO) is very different from traditional SEO. Google heavily favors web pages with YouTube videos embedded in them.

Make sure the thumbnail you have for any video you have posted is attractive and inviting. A still shot from a video with you frowning isn't going to warm your audience up to you. Make sure you have a clear description for your video that would appeal to your prospective reader. Also, be sure you have the appropriate tags and a title for your videos that will attract attention of those people whose attention you want to attract.

Don't ever forget to add your branding to any video that you place on YouTube. Not just in the video itself, but also in the metadata. A viewer may not be on your company's YouTube channel, so make sure that you identify clearly who you are.

Is there an optimal length for a YouTube video? Some will argue that we're a short attention span theater and any of your videos shouldn't be more than a couple minutes. Others will claim that people will watch any length of video and long as it's enjoyable. Even 30 minute long videos have received millions of views.

That being said, if you can say what you need to say in less time then do a shorter video. According to some reports the average video length these days runs about 4.4 minutes.

When you first signup with YouTube your account will be limited to videos less than 15 minutes in length until your account has been "verified." Once your account has been verified, which is relatively simple, you can post any video that isn't greater than 20GB in file size.

The beauty of YouTube is definitely the long shelf life. Almost 40% of a video's views from when it is first posted will happen within the first three weeks, with another 30 percent over the next month. The remaining 30% occurs anywhere between 3 and 12 months out from the release date. So your video continues to work for you long after you've first put it out there.

Some important things to remember:

- In general, shorter is better. But if you need longer to say what needs to be said then go longer.
- Make sure you have great energy right from the beginning of your video and be sure to get the important info in early. For

a 4-5 minute video slightly less than 60% of the viewers will remain until the end. If your video is just 1-2 minutes you'll usually retain around 75%.

- Make sure you have your calls to action in more than one spot in your video and definitely don't wait till the very end only.
- Think about the consumability of the information you want to impart to your audience. If it would be more digestible by breaking it into bite-sized chunks then break it up.
- If the video is of a rousing speech you've done and you'd break the flow by splitting it up then leave it as a longer video, that's fine.

As an author we're usually most comfortable with the written word. But you've got to come out from behind your book and embrace the power of video and of YouTube if you want to increase the impact you'll have with your message. If you're a bit camera shy you'll need to get over it. Certainly it's a skill you get more comfortable with the more often you do it. But, if you truly want to positively influence a greater number of people with your story then your embracing of video will definitely help you down the path to greater success.

> Check out the mistakes Authors Make YouTube channel at YouTube.com/user/MistakesAuthorsMake

Mistake #50

You're Afraid to Give Books Away

E very market promotion you do should be measured. What kind of results did you get for the time and money invested in that promotion? Admittedly, it can be tough to measure sometimes but you certainly need to make the effort.

We talked earlier in the book about how Brendon Burchard built a multi-million dollar business by basically giving his books away. Same for T. Harv Eker. Both of those gentlemen knew their numbers well. They had their back end offers in place and knew the value of each person into whose hands they got their book.

You'll give away your business card to anyone that asks, won't you? So, if your book should be your business card, then why do some authors suddenly get so tight fisted they hang onto their book like it's their last possession in the world?

"Your book should be your business card"

We get that each copy of your books costs you a few dollars. And to go willy nilly out there giving books away without any sense of what you can convert on the back end is a game most of us aren't willing to play. And rightfully so till you really know your numbers well.

But to be so tight fisted you're not willing to give any books away is counterproductive. Your marketing budget should include some figure for giving away books. Only you can decide what that figure should be. And only you can determine the criteria you're going to follow to determine when it is appropriate to give away your books.

When you look at the members of the media you'd like to have on your side or other centers of influence such as key bloggers or possible joint venture partners that can focus more attention on your book then the investment of a few bucks for the gifting of your book makes perfect sense when you've identified who those people are.

Sometimes you'll never know the direct results of each individual copy of your book that you give away. A few years ago Bret recalls giving his book to a very big name marketer. This marketer was doing a weekly online television show that was getting decent viewership. Well, when Bret tuned in each week he found his book prominently displayed on the bookshelves that were the backdrop of the television set. No idea how many books directly sold as a result of being displayed week after week after week. But it didn't hurt any.

Another aspect to the giveaway of books is the whole world of Kindle Direct Publishing. If you are selling your book in Kindle format they allow you to give away your book up to 5 days in every 90-day period. It can be five days in a row or any five days spread out over that 90-day period.

Of course you give up your normal royalties during a period where you're giving away your Kindle version of your book for free. So one might question why you'd want to give your book away on this platform. For some reason, whether it's just due to increased awareness or whatever, authors who give their book away find that the normal sales of their book also increase above their usual numbers after a giveaway period.

So they are willing to give up the royalties of those that take the free offer in exchange for the bump in their regular sales numbers after a giveaway period has ended. And, of course, you still need to factor in the back end value of each person you get your book into the hands of. Maybe some will buy the print version or take you up on some of the other products and/or services you have referenced in your book.

Your book can be the gateway to other things for your readers. Not only can you give away your book, but you can give away things in your book that will lead to the eventual purchase of other things. In T. Harv Eker's book *Secrets of the Millionaire Mind* he gave away tickets to his live event. So he gave away the book to give away event tickets. Seems like a lot of giving away. But he knew once he got them into the room at his event some portion of his original readers who invest in other trainings of his or the products or services of some of his speakers.

Now if you have the kind of bankroll behind you to support this type of approach from the start—wonderful. Go for it if you want to. Certainly most authors don't so you'll need to more selective and possibly more creative on how you're going to approach giveaways. But don't get so tight fisted that you're unwilling to give your book away at all.

You really do need to approach it from the standpoint of being a better business card for you. Your book will give you far more credibility than any 2" x 3" business card ever will. So determine your giveaway budget and your criteria for the giving away of your book and forge ahead. Will you end up giving away some books that don't result in any direct benefit for you? Of course you will. But there will be those select few whose receipt of your book ends up in resulting in far more than you could ever have imagined.

We'd highly encourage you to get on the mailing lists for both Brendon Burchard and T. Harv Eker. Even if you never partake of any of their products and services study the masters. Inspect their business model closely and watch carefully how they do what they do. There's a lot to learn and you're always far better off following the path of someone who has blazed the trail before you.

Conclusion

We hope you've found great benefit from this book and appreciate your investing your time to learn more about the worlds of book marketing and publishing through us. It's such an exciting thing coming out with your book and we're excited for you.

Be sure to take advantage of the many resources mentioned throughout this book that can help you along your path. Don't forget to check out the additional reading and other resources that you can find online at MistakesAuthorsMake.com/resources.

We wish you the greatest of success with your book. You do have a powerful message that should be shared with the world. And, if you're a business owner or business professional you'll find that your book can be the single greatest weapon in your marketing arsenal. Even if you don't write every word yourself get it done – it will pay big dividends for you.

It'll take some work—no doubt about that. But, anything worthwhile always takes some elbow great to make it happen. You can have a powerful impact on the lives of others and the time to go for it is now.

Resources

(For additional resources visit
MistakesAuthorsMake.com/resources)

Author Training

Author101Online.com – On-going training from the book authors to help you keep your positive momentum from this book and between live events. New live trainings twice monthly with our guest experts along with "Ask Rick" calls, a monthly digital newsletter and weekly marketing tips.

Book Cover Design

Kathi Dunn – Dunn-Design.com
Frank Deardurff – IMakeBookCovers.com
Vaughan Davidson – KillerCovers.com

Book Printers
48 Hour Books – 48HourBooks.com
King Printing – KingPrinting.com
Color House Graphics – ColorHouseGraphics.com
Friesens Corp. – Friesens.com
Lightning Source – LightningSource.com
Lulu – Lulu.com
SheridanBooks – SheridanBooks.com
United Graphics – UnitedGraphicsInc.com

Books on Publishing/Book Marketing
Author 101 Bestselling Book Publicity: The Insider's Guide to Promoting Your Book--and Yourself—Rick Frishman, Robyn Freedman Spizman and Mark Steisel

Author 101 Bestselling Book Proposals: The Insider's Guide to Selling Your Work—Rick Frishman and Robyn Freedman Spizman

Author 101 Bestselling Nonfiction: The Insider's Guide to Making Reality Sell—Rick Frishman, Robyn Freedman Spizman and Mark Steisel

Author 101: Bestselling Secrets from Top Agents—Rick Frishman and Robyn Freedman Spizman

Author 101: The Insider's Guide to Publishing From Proposal to Bestseller—Rick Frishman and Robyn Freedman Spizman

Guerrilla Marketing for Writers: 100 No-Cost, Low-Cost Weapons for Selling Your Work—Jay Conrad Levinson, Rick Frishman, Michael Larsen and David Hancock

Write: Why? Marketing for Writers—Kenneth Atchity, Ridgely Goldsborough and Rick Frishman

Show Me About Book Publishing: Survive and Thrive in Today's Literary Jungle—Judith Briles, Rick Frishman and John Kremer

The Entrepreneurial Author: Achieving Success and Balance as a Writer in the 21st Century—David Hancock, Jay Conrad Levinson and Rick Frishman

1001 Ways to Market Your Books—John Kremer

APE: Author, Publisher, Entrepreneur-How to Publish a Book—Guy Kawasaki and Shawn Welch

How to Sell Books by the Truckload on Amazon.com—Book One and Two: Get More Sales—Get More Reviews!—Penny Sansevieri

52 Ways to Sell More Books!— Penny C. Sansevieri

Author YOU-Creating and Building the Author and Book Platforms— Judith Briles

Snappy Sassy Salty: Wise Words for Authors and Writers—Judith Briles

Dan Poynter's Self-Publishing Manual: How to Write, Print and Sell Your Own Book—Dan Poynter

Dan Poynter's Self-Publishing Manual: How to Write, Print and Sell Your Own Book (Volume 2)—Dan Poynter

Writing Nonfiction: Turning Thoughts into Books—Dan Poynter

Writing Your Book—Dan Poynter

CD/DVD Duplication

Speaker Fulfillment Services – Company co-founded by Bret Ridgway and Bryan Hane that works with authors, speakers and information marketers on their products 'beyond the book' like CD and DVD sets, home study courses and more. Visit SpeakerFulfillmentServices.com or call 812-877-7100.

Disc Delivered – Print-on-demand service with your own custom self-mailer for CDs and DVDs. Visit DiscDelivered.com for more information.

Copywriters

Gary Bencivenga – MarketingBullets.com

Bob Bly – Bly.com

John Carlton – John-Carlton.com

Ray Edwards – RayEdwards.com

Michael Fortin – MichelFortin.com

David Garfinkel – DavidGarfinkel.com

Lorrie Morgan-Ferrero – RedHotCopy.com

Copywriting Books

2001 Greatest Headlines Ever Written – Carl Galletti

Advertising Headlines That Make You Rich – David Garfinkel

Breakthrough Advertising – Eugene Schwartz

Breakthrough Copywriting – David Garfinkel

The Copywriter's Handbook – Robert Bly

The First Hundred Million – E. Haldeman-Julius

How to Make Maximum Money in Minimum Time – Gary Halbert

Lazy Man's Guide to Riches – Joe Karbo

MoneyWords – Ray Edwards

My Life in Advertising/Scientific Advertising – Claude Hopkins

Ogilvy on Advertising – David Ogilvy

Quick Start Guide to Writing Red Hot Copy – Lorrie Morgan-Ferrero

Reason Why Advertising Plus Intensive Advertising – John E. Kennedy

Robert Collier Letter Book – Robert Collier

Web Copywriting Secrets from the Trenches – Ray Edwards

Writing Riches – Ray Edwards

Crowdfunding

Pubslush.com

Domain Name Registration
RicksCheapDomains.com

Editors
Amanda Rooker – Split-Seed.com

Email Providers
AWeber.com
GetResponse.com
MailChimp.com
RedOakCart.com

Events
Author 101 University – Author101.com
Author U – AuthorU.org

Ghostwriters
Justin Spizman – JustinSpizman.com

Graphic Artists
Heather Kirk – GraphicsForSuccess.com
Megan Johnson – Johnson2Design.com
Josh Haldeman – TerradiseDesign.com
Vaughan Davidson – KillerCovers.com

ISBN Numbers
Bowker.com

Literary Agents
BruceBarbour.com
FolioLitAgency.com

Media Resources/Training

Gail Kingsbury – InstantMediaKit.com

Starley Murray - StarleyMurray.com

Membership Site Software

Wishlist Member – WishlistMember.com

Merchant Account Providers

PowerPay – InfoMarketingMerchantAccount.com

Order Fulfillment

AuthorFulfillmentServices.com

SpeakerFulfillmentServices.com

Publishers

Morgan James - MorganJamesPublishing.com

Radio Publicity Resources/Training

Alex Carroll – RadioPublicity.com

Shopping Carts

1ShoppingCart.com

Infusionsoft.com

RedOakCart.com

Social Media Managers/Training

Mary Agnes Antonopolous – MaryAgnes.com

Carol McManus – LinkedInLady.com

Melonie Dodaro – TopDogSocialMedia.com

Speaking Training
Wendy Lipton-Dibner – MovePeopleToAction.com

Transcribers
InternetTranscribers.com
SuccessTranscripts.com

Virtual Assistants
FusionOnlineMarketingAgency.com
RheasVAs.com

Warehousing
AuthorFulfillmentServices.com
SpeakerFulfillmentServices.com

Web Hosting
ThatOneHosting.com
LiquidWeb.com

Website Design
21Thirteen.com
PlanetLink.com
TaylorMadeWebPresence.com

Bibliography

http://www.BookPromotionHub.com/6103/How-Many-Books-Do-You-Need-To-Sell-To-Become-A-Bestseller/

http://RadioPublicity.com

http://www.Goodreads.com/blog/show/424-What-Makes-You-Put-Down-A-Book

Scientific Advertising by Claude Hopkins

Ogilvy on Advertising by David Ogilvy

http://www.Goodreads.com/list/show/276.Best_Book_Titles

The First Hundred Million by E. Haldeman-Julius

http://en.wikibooks.org/wiki/basic_book_design/font

ABCs of Speaking by Adryenn Ashley, Bret Ridgway and Caterina Rando

http://www.foliolit.com/resources/writers-conference-etiquette/

http://publishing.about.com/od/bookauthorbasics/a/book-contract-outlined.htm

GKIC No B.S. Marketing Letter, August 2014

http://www.verticalresponse.com/blog/social-media-marketing-
automation-dos-and-donts/

http://www.forbes.com/sites/jeffbercovici/2014/02/10/Amazon-vs-
book-publishers-by-the-numbers/

http://www.USAToday.com/story/life/books/2013/10/06/e-books-
reading/2877471/

http://www.buzzfeed.com/kevintang/late-blooming-artists#1K81XBU

http://www.cms.seahillpress.com/resources/articles/the-reality-of-book-
distribution/

http://SuzyQCoaching.com

http://TheWritersGuideToEPublishing.com/categorizing-your-way-to-
amazons-bestseller-lists-part-one

http://www.copyright.gov/circs/circ15a.pdf

http://www.Lawmart.com/forms/difference.htm

http://AuthorityPublishing.com/book-marketing/how-authors-can-
sell-to-bookstores-free-bookstore-consignment-agreement-for-
authors/

About the Authors

Rick Frishman is the publisher at Morgan James Publishing in New York and founder of Planned Television Arts (now called Media Connect), has been one of the leading book publicists in America for over 35 years. Rick works with many of the top book editors, literary agents, and publishers in America, including Simon and Schuster, Random House, Wiley, Harper Collins, Pocket Books, Penguin Group[and Hyperion Books. He has worked with bestselling authors such as Mitch Albom, Bill Moyers, Stephen King, Caroline Kennedy, Howard Stern, President Jimmy Carter, Mark Victor Hansen, Nelson DeMille, John Grisham, Hugh Downs, Henry Kissinger, Jack Canfield, Alan Deshowitz, Arnold Palmer, and Harvey Mackay.

Morgan James Publishing publishes fiction and nonfiction books and by authors with a platform who believe in giving back. Morgan James gives a portion of every book sold to Habitat for Humanity.

Rick has also appeared on hundreds of radio shows and more than a dozen TV shows nationwide, including *Oprah* and Bloomberg TV. He has also been featured in the *New York Times, Wall Street Journal, Associated Press, Selling Power Magazine, New York Post*, and scores of other publications.

He has appeared on stage with notables such as The Dalai Lama, Sir Richard Branson, T. Harv Eker, Jack Canfield, Mark Victor Hansen, Tony Hsieh, David Bach, Brian Tracy, and Brendon Burchard.

Rick is the coauthor of thirteen books, including national bestsellers *Guerrilla Publicity, Networking Magic, Where's Your Wow* and *Guerrilla Marketing for Writers*. His thirteenth book, *"The 250 Rules of Business"* with coauthor Steven Schragis was published in July of 2013.

Rick has a BFA in acting and directing and a BS in communications from Ithaca College. He is a sought-after lecturer on publishing and public relations and a member of PRSA and the National Speakers Association.

Bret Ridgway is the author or coauthor of 6 books including *The 50 Biggest Mistakes Information Marketers Make, Biggest Website Mistakes Online Business Owners Make* and the upcoming *ABCs of Speaking*. He is co-founder of Speaker Fulfillment Services, an organization that works behind the scenes with authors, speakers and information marketers.

He has worked with many of the biggest names in information marketing, including Armand Morin, Alex Mandossian, Mike Koenigs, Mike Filsaime, Suzanne Evans, Perry Marshall, Ryan Deiss, Alexandria Brown, Frank Kern and *New York Times* bestselling authors Joel Comm and John Assaraf. He is a frequent speaker at live events and on webinars on all aspects of information marketing.

 **Bryan Hane** is a first time coauthor. He is the co-founder with Bret Ridgway of Speaker Fulfillment Services and a founding partner with Rick and Bret of Author 101 Online, a program that provides on-going training and resources for new and experienced authors (more info at Author101Online.com). Bryan is also a founder of Red Oak Cart, a robust ecommerce and email solution. He is an advisor, strategist and marketer for small businesses and has co-founded several successful companies over the last couple decades.

Printed in the USA
CPSIA information can be obtained
at www.ICGtesting.com
JSHW022211140824
68134JS00018B/996

9 781630 474577